INFANT CAREGIVING

a design for training

infant caregiving

a design for training

ALICE S. HONIG

J. RONALD LALLY

SYRACUSE UNIVERSITY PRESS · 1981

CONTENTS

Sensorimotor Period -- 0-2 years
Concrete Operations Period -- 2-11 years
Formal Operations Period -- 11-14 years
Definition of terms

Section II -- Training methods

Training method one: "Example to idea"
Training method two: the "Diagnosis"
  How the caregiver learns to make good matches
  Ways to end learning games happily
Training method three: the "Discovery"
Training method four: "Make-up-a-game"

Feeding space
Toileting space
Storage space
Room furnishings: for play, for privacy
Book places
Sleep space
Crib and wall decor
Mirrors
Rug-and-furniture-defined play areas
Taking advantage of other room features
Keeping living spaces and toys clean and safe
A place for sick babies
A space for living and growing creatures
Using the Day Care building for adventures
Visits with other infants
Visiting other Day Care Center Personnel
Visiting special center areas
Outdoor worlds to conquer

Who does what?
How are babies assigned to a caregiver?
Who keeps records? What kinds of records need to be
    kept?
What are trainees' responsibilities when they are not
    on the job?
What clothes do we wear as caregivers?
How and when do the infants go on trips away from the
    Center?
What are the caregivers' rights and responsibilities
    with regard to outsiders?
When and how do we get together with parents?
Whom does a caregiver see when he or she has a problem?
How do Day Care Center days begin and end?

Section I -- What we have learned about infant
    caregiving

PREFACE TO THE SECOND EDITION

The decade since publication of the first edition of <u>Infant Caregiving</u> has witnessed an urgent national need for quality group care for children under the age of three. Increasing numbers of single parents and working parents seek such care. This national need can be met — if enough caregivers are well prepared to love and to cherish, to teach and to delight in the babies and toddlers entrusted to their care.

Infants flourish when special people are sensitive to them and can meet their needs. Such special people can provide babies with living, loving, and learning experiences that promote competence and kindness, curiosity and cooperation, resourcefulness, purposeful persistence, affection, and joy. Special people can assist babies to acquire information about the surrounding physical and social world, to acquire more mature ways of communicating, and to learn effective ways to make things happen in their environment.

Those who are trainers of infant caregivers will need to encourage special skills in the adults who are learning. <u>Infant Caregiving</u> has been specifically designed as a resource for trainers. Many areas of knowledge and know-how have a chapter of their own. Chapters 9 and 10 address a variety of topics as well as plans for later in-service training. In this edition, a new Chapter 11 covers special topics such as assessment of caregiver skills and of infant development, infant sexuality, and communicating with parents. The greatly expanded reference section increases a trainer's options for choosing textual and audiovisual resources to help in the training program.

A person who wants to become a quality infant caregiver deserves the highest quality of training. The context of training is crucial. How the trainer uses personal resources and materials will strongly influence the course and outcome of the training program. While using this book, a trainer may refer to the following list of maxims to enhance the adventure which trainer and trainees will embark upon together.

Twenty Tips for Trainers of Infant Caregivers

1. Communicate clearly basic information about how babies grow and how adults facilitate that growth.

2. Model the behaviors that you want caregivers to exhibit. Don't just talk about what you would like to see. Show how.

3. Skills grow through practice permeated by understanding. Make sure that caregivers see how techniques and methods they are to use in interactions with babies depend upon information.

4. Treat experts as consultants. Treat texts and audiovisual materials as resources. Neither are infallible.

5. Explore with caregivers their feelings about freely offering physical cuddling, holding, and stroking. How comfortable are caregivers about freely accepting a baby's need to nuzzle, to drape, to lean, sometimes to cling? Babies need physical validation of their goodness. Delight and comfort with their bodies is tied to delight in themselves.

6. Have caregivers talk about their beliefs and ideas about what is best for young children. Some adults hold strong beliefs that are not compatible with optimal child development

practices. Some of these nonproductive beliefs are: "If you pick up a baby you will spoil her." "A boy needs to fight to learn to be a man." "Clean diapers and a bottle once in a while are all babies really need."

Which beliefs of trainees are supported by research findings? Which may need further discussion because they could result in insensitive or sexist interactions with tots?

7. Have caregivers clarify their values and decide which are the most important and least important. A value is a judgment of "good" or "bad." Probe for value conflicts. For example, does a trainee believe that child competence gained through slow or messy or clumsy trying is important but that adult convenience when caring for a group of children is even more important? Is early potty-training more important than safeguarding the toddler's sense of self-esteem and rights to gain self-control at a pace that protects his or her self-confidence?

Children catch the unconscious as well as the conscious values of adults who rear them. Which highly valued characteristics will the children interpret as important from your trainees -- compassion, fairness, and patience or convenience and conformity?

8. Explore goals for infant caregivers. Relate the goals of training to beliefs and to values. Learning to care for others and learning to learn are two important goals. Have caregivers encourage and model their social goals and their problem-solving goals in interactions with babies. Have caregivers share their images and visions of how they think they are going to be when the training is over. Stimulate awareness of change.

9. Take the contributions and questions of participants in the training session seriously. Expose blame or ridicule as useless for adults and for children. Teach trainees how to use "I" statements to communicate their feelings and wishes in training sessions and in order to let small children know adults' wishes and wants. Teach "You" statements which help an adult communicate that the adult acknowledges and validates the child's distressed or happy feelings (see Chapter 11).

10. Be open to mistakes in training. Redefine failure so that risks are taken. Learning is a risky venture. Trainers and trainees can risk, try out, learn, fail, and continue to grow to become quality caregivers, openly, together. None of us can be a "perfect" caregiver. We strive toward excellence. The road to excellence is strewn with mistakes made along the way.

11. Revise your training emphases and attention to topic areas based on what you learn during training sessions and from reading diary feedback from the trainees.

12. Increase caregiver noticing skills. Without sensitive observation skills it is difficult to interpret and apply new knowledge aptly and appropriately with young children. Trainees need to listen with new ears, see with new eyes, feel into the feelings of young ones.

13. Set up a context for cooperative care. Caregivers can find ways to help each other help babies to flourish.

14. Emphasize the ways in which caregivers can embed curricular goals and activities as well as positive ways of being attuned to young children, into daily routines and necessary "housekeeping" chores.

15. Language is a wondrous power. Encourage trainees to express themselves in sessions with babies, with parents, with

each other. Model songs, chants, rhymes, and word games. Help trainees rejoice in their own use of language power as they help babies gain mastery in understanding and using language.

16. Search for caregiver strengths. As you train, watch for growth in understanding and in adeptness. Praise sincerely. Praise specifically.

17. Get something out of the training for yourself. Learn more about yourself in the process of teaching and helping others to learn. Share yourself -- your feelings, your successes, your failures in interactions. Mutually satisfying cycles of giving and getting are the foundation of a baby's positive emotional sturdiness. Interchanges of giving and getting will add to your own positive energetic feelings.

18. There is no one single way to train or to become a quality caregiver. Use a variety of techniques. Honor individual differences. Encourage creativity and thoughtful choices in presenting new materials, arranging learning environments, handling inappropriate behaviors, facilitating loving encounters, and luring a baby into trying somewhat challenging tasks.

19. Expand your expectations of caregivers as training progresses. Tell the truth gently, matter-of-factly, consistently. Create a climate for human and professional blossoming. Becoming an excellent caregiver is an adventure in personal growth.

20. Foster spiritually sustaining qualities -- compassion, a sense of stirred wonder, doses of humor to relieve tedium or tumbles, comradely courtesies, and joy in the adventure of living and developing.

Spring 1981   ASH/JRL

INTRODUCTION

Growth of individual trainees is the goal of any successful training experience. Growth, however, is a very general term, and often it has been defined too narrowly. Trainers are, in a very real sense, responsible for changing the lives of people in their programs, and to have a truly effective training program, the needs of the trainees must be considered as well as the needs of the trainers and their programs. "The growing self," says Earl Kelley, "must feel that it is involved, that it is really part of what is going on, that in some degree it is helping shape its own destiny, together with the destiny of all." We feel that this kind of involvement should be a goal of training.

Trainers should be aware of the effect they are having on the self-image of the trainees and how important a positive self-image is to the successful functioning of any worker. The ways trainers and others in the learning environment treat the learner is crucial. Growth does not come completely from the mastery of skills, the acquisition of knowledge or the understanding of strategies.

PEOPLE LEARN THEY HAVE ABILITY NOT BY FAILING, BUT BY SUCCEEDING.

The creation of a climate of trust and openness and the recognition of the worth of individual trainees are also central to growth. Intertwining this broad definition of growth with the creation of an atmosphere of mutual involvement makes training a much more complex but meaningful task. It is therefore important to choose carefully the people who will become trainers. Consider carefully the needs and motives of people applying for training positions and select only those who **are at ease with themselves and feel secure enough with trainees.**

Trainees reach many people with their ideas: They benefit directly from their work, of course, and so do the children to whom they give care; but they also affect, indirectly, the family members -- children and adults -- related both to the trainees and to the children served by the caregiving facilities. Although the job may be difficult, it should prove very rewarding when trainers consider the far-reaching effects of their work. They are changing their communities, as well as serving community needs (working parents of young children often are in great need of day care facilities with skilled, competent and trained personnel). It is a job in which they can take pride and satisfaction.

Of critical importance to the success of a training program are the preconceptions of the program director and trainers toward the people they select. If the director and trainers believe that they are selecting the best people for a job, the chances for a successful training program will increase. However, if they are selecting trainees because they are cheaper, because they want to keep peace in the inner city or because they have a local guideline with which they would like to comply, then no matter how they use the materials and ideas available to them they will probably fail. It is not enough, then, to make use of the methods, materials and strategies presented in this handbook. One must remember that the trainee's view of the ways she has been accepted and viewed by the people running the program will have a great deal to do with her becoming an effective child care worker.

The child has contact with all workers in a child care facility -- cooks, custodial workers, drivers, riders, secretaries and receptionists. We recommend that these people participate in the training sessions as often as possible so that they and the caregivers on the staff will treat children in a similar fashion. Children identify with and imitate the people with whom they become familiar. In most child care facilities the children become familiar with everyone. We do not mean by this that everyone should be a caregiver. Secretaries need to know how to type, and cooks must be able to prepare tasty and attractive meals. But if the cook receives training in child care, then you can broaden her role and make it more appealing to her while making her more appealing to the children. For example (from Parker and Dittman):

> *The food service worker no longer operates in the limited confines of the kitchen but expands her role into the program and into the lives of the families.*
>
> *She plans and develops programs that involve children*

9

learning through foods and/or through mealtimes. It is she who introduces concepts like hard and soft, and sweet and sour. She exposes the children to foods in the different forms. She lets the child see grapes turn to raisins and helps the child change apples into applesauce. She helps the children understand that the same foods can look completely different at different times. For example, a jack-o-lantern is a pumpkin and can later be eaten. She takes the child to the supermarket and lets him see what goes on in the store behind the scene. She helps the children plant gardens, takes them to farms, canneries, etc., and allows them to prepare various dishes. All of the foregoing can take place within her continual responsibility to serve foods that come from the child's ethnic background, while, at the same time, she introduces foods from other groups...

Additionally, the food service worker plays an important role with parents as she uses her skills to build upon the knowledge of the parents through help with budgeting, shopping information, and new food preparations.

This book is definitely not a "how-to" approach to training. There are many ways that one can train an effective child care worker and our approach is certainly not the only way one can do it. But one of the interesting observations we have come to make about training programs is that the somewhat intangible, emotional feelings of worth and the individual's positive feeling about his ability to do a job are dynamics difficult to program and often come to the caregiver from the trainer-trainee relationship during the training period, not from the training manual.

The question-and-answer style which we have used throughout the text allows us to put down on paper all our information, but we do not advise the trainer to use only this technique.

Role playing, for example, small group discussions, psycho-
drama, actual experiences with babies, mothers and materials,
and many other techniques enrich the training process and
increase its effectiveness.

We have used specific examples from the setting with which we
are most familiar, the day care center. More appropriate
textual phrasing would have been "child care facility" which
can include, in addition to day care center, family day care
homes, institutions for child care, nursery schools, camps and,
of course, private homes. However, we feared that we would
lose some of the exactness of our illustrations if we used so
general a term as "child care facility."

We have limited this training handbook to the infancy period,
but have used a new and increasingly popular definition of
that period, which includes children* from birth to 36 months
of age. This broader age range lets us include information
for all children up to the "preschool age" (usually thought of
as three to five years). We have not discussed in detail many
areas that are very important to successful child care, for
example, the health and nutritional needs of young children and
the information their caregivers should possess about these
subjects. Nor have we given detailed instructions on custodial

*Additionally, for clarity of presentation, we have adopted
the convention of designating all these children as males,
and all caregivers as females. It is, of course, considered
highly desirable that caregivers and infants of both sexes
be present to enhance and enrich the learning and living
experiences of the day care program.

techniques and routines such as how to fold or change a diaper, prepare a bath, or warm up portions of strained infant food. We have not discussed exhaustively those considerations of which a caregiver should be fully aware, such as the culture from which a child comes. We have not discussed extensively the record-keeping nor the personal contacts between staff members that are an important part of a child care worker's daily activities. We have focused on the child development aspects of training and have left some of those other very important areas to those who are better qualified.

A final practical suggestion to people planning to use this handbook as a guide for training: Keep, or have a member of your staff keep, a careful diary of the training program. Note particularly the suggestions that trainees make in the various topical areas and their responses to different training techniques you use and materials you present. Not only can this diary be used with your materials by the trainee when she has finished the training program, but it can also be used directly by the trainer to make future training sessions more effective. Diaries are invaluable aids in evaluating pre-service programs and in planning your in-service program. Diaries help you write, in effect, your own training handbook.

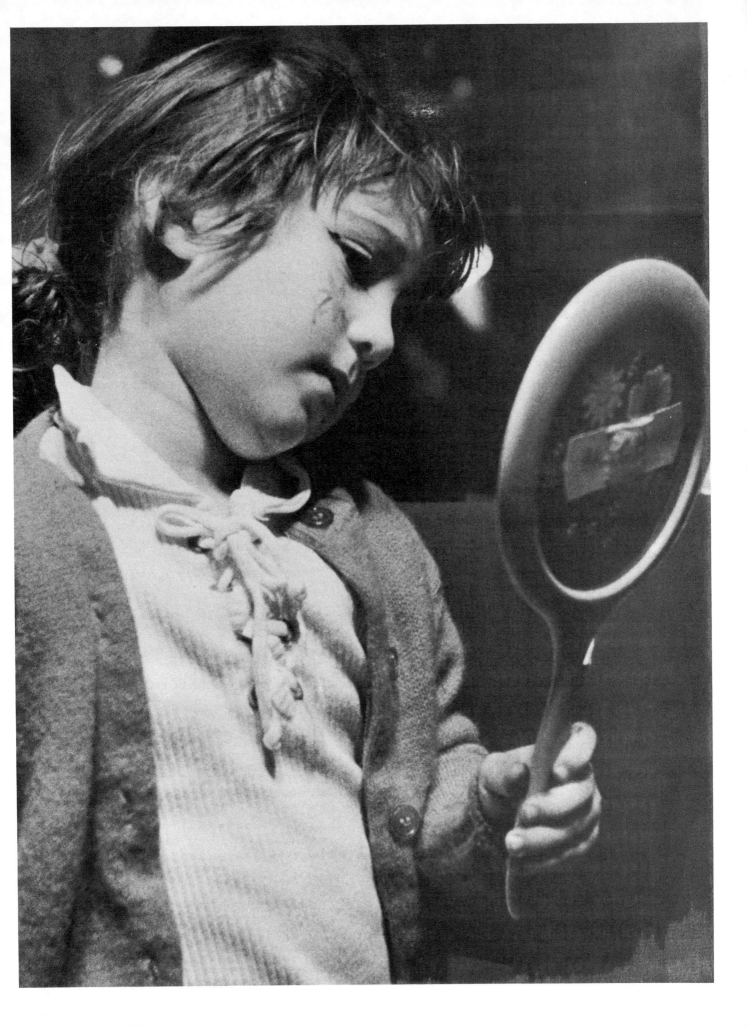

1

DEVELOPING A HEALTHY PERSONALITY

Emotional development in infancy and how a caregiver can help promote a healthy personality in her infants can be covered in a series of short conversations* with trainees. Sandwich these discussions between sessions on large-muscle skill games or on infant language, for example. Breaking up the emotional health material gives trainees a better chance to digest some of the concepts you are introducing. Some of the trainees may have shown a lack of patience for their own children's clumsy or unsuccessful efforts to learn new skills or more acceptable behaviors. In introducing ways to develop an

USE CONCRETE EXAMPLES OF OBSERVED TRAINEE-INFANT OR MOTHER-INFANT INTERACTIONS FROM THE OTHER SESSIONS TO HELP YOU ILLUSTRATE IDEAS ABOUT HOW ADULTS CAN HELP PROMOTE A HEALTHY PERSONALITY IN BABIES.

affectionate and sensitive appreciation of babies and to handle discipline problems, you will have to be careful not to make trainees feel that the methods they may have used with their own youngsters were "all wrong."

---

*Also use four films, prepared by Dr. L. J. Stone of Vassar College, which are available from the Modern Talking Picture Service, 1212 Avenue of the Americas, New York, N.Y. These films are very appropriate for training since they show caregivers who are effective and others who are inadequate in promoting good emotional growth in infants. The films are: *Person to Person in Infancy, Emotional Ties in Infancy, Psychological Hazards in Infancy,* and *Learning to Learn in Infancy.* The latter film emphasizes the Piagetian notion of the role of curiosity and exploration in infant learning.

Goals

Your goals here are to help trainees

➤ understand emotional development in infancy, and

➤ find ways to get a baby to enjoy himself and to

feel comfortable and competent with his caregivers

and his world of food, toys, people and places.

What the young baby takes in with his mouth, his body and his hands should feel good to him. What he takes in with his eyes should be interesting to him.*

The Importance Of Trainer Feedback To Trainees

An important part of your training procedure must include being alert during all the other training sessions when a trainee at any time behaves with a baby in such a fashion as to promote

➤ his competence,

➤ good feelings about himself,

➤ friendly actions toward the

people around him.

*G*UARD AGAINST THE ASSUMPTION THAT BECAUSE TRAINEES MAY NOD AFFIRMATIVELY AS YOU TALK ABOUT NEW WAYS OF DISCIPLINE THAT THEY AGREE WITH YOUR IDEAS.

Make sure you praise the trainee for

*Appropriate readings: Erikson (Chapter 7, "The Eight Ages of Man," pp. 247-274); Escalona (pp. 7-12); Stone & Church ("The Infant," pp. 56-163; and "The Toddler," pp. 222-273); Appendix B of *The Training of Family Day Care Workers* (Dokecki, et al.; will help you teach the use of positive reinforcement techniques to manage behavior).

her specific gestures and words.*

DO NOT ASSUME THAT TRAINEES WILL BE ABLE TO FIND GOOD WAYS TO CARRY OUT YOUR IDEAS IN ACTUAL, OFTEN STRESSFUL, DISCIPLINE SITUATIONS.

Awareness Of Individual Differences

Your first conversations will explore the growth of basic trust or mistrust in infancy and the differences among infants in their needs. Have the trainees describe as many physical and psychological needs of an infant as they can. They should mention needs for food, sleep, cuddling, non-nutrituve sucking, warmth, body-cleaning and interesting play and talk. Some babies can wait patiently for a while in a crib until a caregiver comes to change and feed them. Others howl despairingly for food immediately on awakening from sleep. Make sure that the trainees understand that not all babies have these needs with the same

BABIES DIFFER IN TEMPERAMENT AND ACTIVITY LEVEL.

intensity or frequency. Some babies need a lot more sleep or sucking than others. Some need a lot more rocking or bodily soothing to get calm. Get the trainees to tell you stories about their own or their friend's babies who have shown these

{ *See Beller, pp. 229-265. }

16

very different patterns of need.

Agree with the trainees if they remark that it is not always an easy task for a caregiver to find the key to comforting a distressed baby. But all babies need a good amount of satisfaction of their needs in order to learn that the world is a good place in which to be born and to live. How and what caregivers do to handle infant frustrations and discomforts matters very much. Loving and prompt responses to infant needs teach the baby his distress is not overwhelming because caregivers can be trusted to bring comfort and help to him. When caregivers do not meet enough of a baby's needs, the frustrated baby develops a basic mistrust of the world and his own ability to cope with it or to learn in it.

Consistent Care And The Growth Of Trust

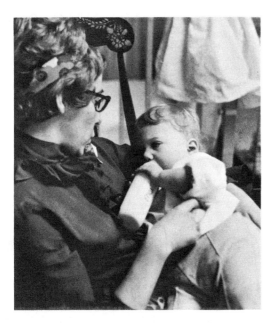

Babies who have regularly experienced long delays in gratification of their needs or inconsistencies in gratification may develop unhappy feelings about people and life. Their faces often look sad or fretful or apathetic or anxious. A caregiver who is responsible for such an infant may have to give extra doses of consistent attention and care so that her infant learns slowly that she is his special person. He can trust her. She will not let him cry until he reaches a state of rage or panic. She will vary his position frequently, keep him comfortable, and provide him with loving and interesting experiences. Provide some large dolls and ask the trainees to show you how they would rub a baby's back, put him to shoulder, stroke his tummy while diapering him, nuzzle his neck or his toes while playing with him. Ask the trainees at what age babies stop needing physical cuddling or loving. Praise them for observing that most people at all ages need some physical expressions of affection. A hug and a proud pat or grin of approval or admiration is a prescription whose dosage may differ for different babies, but which babies and toddlers need in order to thrive. Ask the trainees what kinds of hints a baby might give to show that his caregiver had established this basic relation of trust with him. They may remark that such a baby may smile a greeting to her when she comes into his room. He may stretch his arms to her in order to be comforted if he bumps himself. If he is frightened by a new loud toy, he may run and hang onto her skirt. When asked to play sociable games by a stranger he may stare suspiciously, and yet enter with pleasure into a game with his caregiver.

Toward the end of Caldwell's film, *How Babies Learn*, which you will show during the language sessions to teach trainees about infant-adult conversations, there is a good sequence illustrating the basic trust relationship. A strange lady tries

18

to coax the infant to come to her. The baby's face is sober,

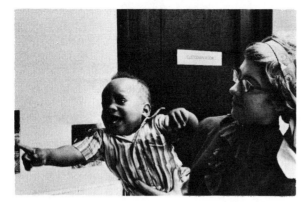 

hesitant or alarmed. Yet as soon as the mother picks up her
infant lovingly and securely in her arms, the baby boy is able
to turn and give the "stranger" a warm smile.

Somewhere about 6 to 8 months, some babies develop, for shorter
or longer periods, what is called "separation anxiety." They
are upset if their special person disappears even for a little
while. Ask the trainees in what sense this can be considered
a positive emotional sign in a baby.
The trainees who have seen the mother-
abandoned infant in Caldwell's film
going from one set of arms to
another, indifferent to whose they
might be, will be quick to note that
such responses tell that this
baby has not developed a special
relationship of attachment to a
caregiver.

*B*ABIES WHO HAVE STRONG
POSITIVE ATTACHMENTS
TO A CAREGIVER HAVE
BEEN FOUND TO
DEVELOP CONCEPTS
SUCH AS "OBJECT
PERMANENCE" EARLIER
AND FASTER.

Timing

Talk with the trainees about the importance of timing and of intensity of their emotional input to a baby. Ask them these questions: "When a baby has just woken up from a nap, is it a good time for loud laughing play?" "If a baby has <u>just</u> begun to concentrate on a new problem which is hard for him (such as searching for the right size hole for a peg), is that a good time to give him non-stop lavish praise for his accomplishments?" "If a baby has been using the potty pretty regularly for a few days, is that a good reason to decide that encouraging comments about his actions are no longer necessary?"

What "No-no" Means

Explore with the trainees what happens to the infant's sense of "trust" if someone says "No-no" to him frequently. The caregiver should feel competent about handling, bathing, soothing, playing with and enjoying an infant. If she says "No-no" very often, or calls out long-distance warnings like, "Get your hands out of that drawer," she is showing the infant she does not trust his early efforts at exploring or mastering his environment.

TRUST IS A FOUR-WAY CONCEPT. THE BABY LEARNS TO TRUST CAREGIVERS AND HIS OWN GROWING ABILITY TO COPE WITH HIS BODY'S FUNCTIONS AND A WORLD FULL OF EXPLORABLE THINGS. THE CAREGIVER MUST SHOW TRUST IN HERSELF AND ALSO IN HER INFANT.

The infant may not understand the words telling him to stop
his actions. Long-distance warnings, threats and prohibitions
are not an effective way for babies to learn what is unsafe
or unsuitable. Make a list of a series of such potential
situations in a nursery. Get each trainee to talk about one
such situation. Ask them for other ways to cope with behaviors
which are to be discouraged. Praise
trainee suggestions that involve
coming over and carrying out an
action that will help a baby to
comprehend a "No-no" situation such

STRESS THE PREVENTION,
WHERE POSSIBLE, AND
CIRCUMVENTION OF
DANGEROUS SITUATIONS.

as poking fingers in a drawer while trying to shut the drawer.
Very young babies should not have access to open electric plugs,
for example. Ask the trainees to use brief explanations when
a firm prohibition is necessary with an energetic toddler who
is into or onto everything.

The Distraction Technique

Describe the use of distraction techniques. A baby who is
creeping toward a toy in which another infant is attentively
absorbed may be offered an equally attractive toy for himself.
The alert caregiver can avoid potentially distressing
situations for infants if she is a good observer of the
cruising or reaching infant. Sometimes simply starting an
interesting sociable game like pat-a-cake can distract a baby
who is reaching to pull down the attractive-looking bibs on a

21

drying rack.

The Need For Grasping And Biting

Toward the end of the first year of life, babies have definite grasping and biting needs. How can a caregiver help baby to express these needs with least hurt to himself and others? The trainees may suggest the use of teething toys, teething biscuits and plenty of graspable toys rather than, for instance, hair to pull.

Scolding: A Negative Reinforcer

When a young baby bites or strikes another, the injured baby can often be attended to without giving undue attention to the biter. Scolding is attention, negative as it may be, directed to the biting baby. A lot of attention, given promptly and consistently after a person's *PROMPT ATTENTION IS A POWERFUL REINFORCER OF ACTIONS, BOTH POSITIVE AND NEGATIVE.* actions, tends to increase the chances for that action to be repeated. Ask the trainees what they may have noticed about children who receive frequent scoldings (negative attention). Have they noticed how often such a child seems to ignore the scolding and carry out the behavior again and again? Ask the trainees: "What does the scolding parent generally do then?" Often the exasperated parent escalates his response. A louder scolding, more frequent yelling, seem necessary to stop,

22

even for a little while, the disapproved behavior. "Putting a child down" by scolding or shaming him is an inefficient method to manage behavior. It exhausts and irritates a caregiver and makes a child nervous or fearful or defiantly angry. Scolding is <u>not</u> to be confused with an adult's not accepting a baby's action. For example, an adult may firmly tell a toddler, "I don't like to be kicked. Kicking hurts me. I do not want you to kick me."

Physical Punishment

Physical punishment, too, may initially stop a baby's actions. Ask the trainees: "In the long run, what does the baby learn from being hit?" He learns from his caregiver to be a giver of hits! His disapproved behaviors may grow more, not less, frequent as he grows older. As with scoldings, physical punishments may have to be made more and more severe by parents as the child grows older in order to stop the behavior even momentarily. Caregivers who use physical punishment a good deal usually generate more anger and aggressive behavior in their youngsters, even though these outbursts may take place at later times and other places.

Use Positive Reinforcers

The use of positive rather than negative-oriented expressions can be very helpful in returning an infant to more acceptable behaviors. "We need to pour water into the <u>pail</u>," or, "Let's

23

rock Angela more <u>gently</u> in her chair," are preferable to, "Don't spill the water on the floor," or, "Stop rocking Angela so hard; you're hurting her."

Help the caregivers see that using positive methods aids behavior management. Get them to encourage such behaviors as a baby reaching to pat another's hair gently, a

__P__ROMPT POSITIVE ATTENTION CAN INCREASE A BEHAVIOR THE ADULT FINDS DESIRABLE.

baby lifting his arm to help the caregiver who is clothing him, a baby holding his cup steadily as he drinks and spills very

little of his juice. Stress the varieties of attention which an adult might give. Exposure to all kinds of positive input is good for babies. There is no one formula for loving. The more love, genuine enjoyment and approval the

caregiver has shown in her relation to the infant, the more he can trust her judgement about

__E__ACH CAREGIVER HAS HER OWN SPECIAL WAY OF BEING ATTENTIVE.

➤ what things are dangerous to play with,

➤ what new experiences he should try (such as the strange taste of a metallic spoon with a bit of cereal), or

➤ what discomforts (such as a visit to the doctor for a shot) can be borne without undue terrors if she is there to reassure him.

Independence And Initiative:

What Baby Should Gain In His Next Two Stages Of Growth

Erikson's concept of how a healthy personality grows begins with the first critical struggle of infancy: The establishment of basic trust. Your talks started with this stage. Now progress along Erikson's lines, to the next two important problems to be resolved by older infants and preschoolers: Namely, the baby's struggle for independence and later his problems in developing initiative to make choices and decisions of his own.

As his body muscles grow sturdier and he gains more control over them, an infant strives to do more things for himself, to assert his own needs and wants. He is still quite dependent on his caregivers. If they ridicule his early efforts to assert his will or to try out new behaviors, even if his efforts are clumsy or impulsive, then he may be beset by feelings of shame or doubt about himself. Caregivers need to respect baby's early efforts at establishing his rights to be treated fairly as a person. Caregivers, by respecting a baby's wants, teach him more socially acceptable ways of living and help the baby feel more secure about his abilities to express his needs and to have a say in the activities he carries out.

Point out to the trainees that each of the problems of mental health which Erikson says must be resolved during the eight stages of man are all interrelated and all exist in some form in early infancy. Yet each stage of growth involves a

25

special emphasis on solving one of the life problems. The first task of early infancy is the baby's learning to develop a basic sense of trust rather than mistrust toward the persons in his world. A negative example would be the very young infant who turns his head away if a caregiver washes his face too roughly. He is asserting his needs. A satisfactory solution to any one of Erikson's basic life problems will, in part, depend on a good developmental outcome for the growing person as he struggles with each problem in turn.

Trainees Role-Play

How They Help Babies To Develop A Healthy Personality

Prepare a set of "situations" involving the toddler trying to move (walk or jump or ride or climb), to handle objects (lift something heavy or awkward to carry), or to carry out his own body functions (toileting or dressing). Ask each trainee to describe how she might handle a baby whose wills are mighty but whose skills are weak at this stage. Have trainees in pairs act out these situations. Make sure the trainee playing "baby" acts impulsively sometimes -- throwing a toy, running into a table edge, or clutching a metal toy when her caregiver wants her to give it up at nap time. As you watch each caregiver handling her "baby" in the situation being acted out, discuss such situations with each other. Ask the trainees: "How does a caregiver provide the protections required by the young explorer while 'trusting' him enough so he can gain experience with climbing or dressing himself?" Be sure you stress the following ideas during the role-playing sessions, all of which encourage mastery of skills and independence:

- Provision of strategic help which is not perceived by baby as intruding on his vigorous attempts to "help" himself.

- Provision of environmental aids (such as 3-step set of climbing stairs).

- Not using shaming words or words that cast doubt on the child's competence.

- Provision of materials manageable by the toddler -- a two- or three-piece puzzle rather than a ten-piece one, a small set of stacking blocks rather than very large bulky ones, or a painting apron that slips on just with waist clasps; forcing a baby to meet a life challenge, such as toileting only in places and at times acceptable to an adult, before his own body and muscles are ready to cope with this problem, may make him reject the notion that what others want of him and what he wants for himself can agree easily in his life.

- Knowing when not to help.

Ask the trainees to explain what is happening if a toddler takes his sneakers on and off over and over again. Can they accept that this is his way of showing "Me do it!" as so many toddlers proclaim to overly-helpful parents. The wise caregiver accepts a baby's need to try for himself -- and try and try again. This can be an exasperating period for a caregiver. Dawdling babies need a caregiver's patience. Learning when to help or not to help, how much to help, how to give a reassuring smile or an encouraging nod to a baby trying a new skill, is an important skill for a caregiver. Her

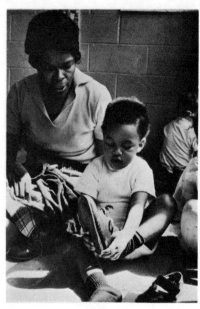

composure, her patient voice tones, her
sensitivity to the toddler's difficult
times and her willingness to let him
learn in his own style will help the
baby through this period. Trainees
also need to understand how much a baby
still needs her during this period. A
trusted, loved caregiver is a secure
base to return to when explorations
become too frustrating or fatiguing.

Perspective and a sense of humor help the caregiver during
times when a baby, his desires and abilities still far apart,
struggles to act independently and to carry out his own wants.
A sense of humor also helps the caregiver to separate larger
power struggles (such as the toddler who wants to run into
the street after a ball) from minor negativisms. Many a
toddler has shaken his head with violent "No-no-no" to the
suggestion that he begin to put toys away because lunch is
just about ready. Almost immediately thereafter, the toddler,
smelling the odor of a favorite food, may run in, climb into
his chair and demand his meal right away. The toddler's
thrust forward into the brave new world of autonomy is neither
consistent nor total. The caregiver who is comfortable with
her own reasonable judgements will more easily manage the
difficulties of the toddler period. Keeping a calm tempo to
the day, accepting baby's see-sawing bouts of boldness and

timidity, and enjoying his smallest steps forward in new
accomplishments with him will foster the healthy personality
development of an infant.

2
THE YOUNG INFANT AND HOW HE GROWS: Nutrition

Enjoying feedings, using his limbs and body in an increasing variety of actions, developing more precise finger and hand skills, and experiencing comfort and delight from sensory experiences are basic to an infant's healthy and happy growth. You will need several sessions to cover these four areas of development. These areas are more usually defined as nutrition, gross and fine motor skills, and sensory activities.

Because the new trainee will probably already be comfortable with the notion that what a baby eats and how he enjoys his eating are important to his development, it is easy to begin with nutrition when you are teaching about physical growth and development.*

Sucking

Ask the trainees what action of a very young baby they would

---

*For infant feeding practices and foods for infants, see Keister, pp. 33-46. For pediatric advice on infant feeding, see Spock and Lowenberg. For available free folders on foods and feeding young children, see: *Baby's Eating and Sleeping Habits*, Johnson & Johnson. *Feeding Your Baby At Your Breast*, National Dairy Council. *When Your Baby Is Bottle Fed*, National Dairy Council. *Food For Your Baby's First Year*, U. S. Government Printing Office, 1969. *Feeding Your Baby During His First Year*, National Dairy Council. *Foods for the Preschool Child*, U. S. Government Printing Office. *Foods Before Six*, National Dairy Council. *Food for the Family with Young Children*, U. S. Department of Agriculture.

choose as the <u>most</u> important for him. They will probably all agree on sucking. Talk with the trainees about a baby's strong need to suck for food (when hungry), for comfort (when tired, for example), and just for the sheer pleasure of sucking. Sucking nourishes more than the infant's body. His mouth is baby's first way to explore the world. By sucking on all kinds of objects he learns about them -- which are good to taste and eat (the nipple from which his milk flows), and which calm him down (his thumb, his rubber toys).

If your day care center is integrated into a factory or work setting, some of the infants' mothers may be coming in to nurse their babies. You will want to talk about breast-feeding and how the caregiver can be helpful to the mother. She can be careful not to give formula between feedings. Providing water or juice in bottles can help tide a fretful baby over the hour until the nursing mother arrives. Changing the baby before he is nursed will help him settle down to suckling more comfortably.

For the bottle-fed babies in the Center, a variety of formulae may be prescribed by the pediatrician. Display some of the kinds of ingredients to be used. If there is a staff member solely responsible for food preparation, she can be asked to talk about infant formulae. What to feed a colicky or an allergic

FOR A BABY, THE RELATION BETWEEN FOOD AND THE FEEDING PERSON IS ONE OF THE STRONGEST BONDS A CAREGIVER CAN ESTABLISH.

32

baby is important. Just as important is <u>how</u> he is fed his milk. Ask the trainees about various ways in which a baby can be fed. They will probably mention bottle-propping in the crib as a frequently-used method. If a caregiver cuddles a baby for bottle feeding, he will have a natural and easy way of learning day after day whom to "trust" for food and the pleasures of his all-important sucking needs. When baby is fed will also affect his developing sense of trust in the adults who care for him. Some newborn babies need to nurse every two or three hours. Many babies are content with longer times between feedings. Make sure the trainees understand that young babies need to be fed when they are hungry and not at fixed times which may be more convenient for an adult.

Solid Foods

When should baby be fed solid foods? When should one switch from strained to table foods? Babies differ in the ages at which they become able to digest different kinds of foods. Some also have difficulty in adjusting to the strange taste of a metal spoon or a plastic cup. Home-mashed applesauce may taste very odd to baby compared to the familiar, easy to manage, commercial strained food. Some babies grow very rapidly and need the extra energy that cereal and strained fruits provide as early as eight weeks. Talk about differences in the growth rates and activity levels of babies.* Food

{ *Mussen, Conger and Kagan, pp. 145-148 and 199-203. }

needs will vary sharply with growth patterns and with individual needs. Weight gains slow down in the second year from the birthweight tripling which occurs during the first year of life. Babies by the end of the first year <u>may</u> be on three meals a day with snacks at mid-morning and mid-afternoon. Some babies at that age still need night nursing. Others can easily go without a night feeding.

Nutrition: Displays And Demonstrations

Spend some time demonstrating the kinds of infant food available in jars and how to warm and serve this food. Discuss the size of food portions appropriate for babies of different sizes and appetites. Later on, during the motor-skills sessions, you may invite guest mothers and babies to stay for lunch. Schedule such lunch hours when possible so that trainees can practice preparing food, feeding infants and observing mothers feed their infants.

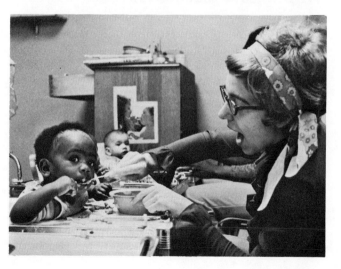

Meal times with trainees offer a good opportunity for you to set out nutrition displays. Show pictures of caregivers feeding babies nutritionally-balanced snacks for meals and pictures of infants feeding themselves safe, colorful snacks appropriate for different-aged infants. Display some pictures of caregivers using feeding times to promote sociable relations among infants and toddlers. For example, a caregiver and toddlers can chat together and munch on thin slices of an apple which the caregiver slowly peels, slices and serves to each child and to herself at snack time. Include some birthday party pictures of toddlers enjoying with each other the special foods and special events of the party.

Meals: A Social Time

For solid food feeding of the baby who is able to sit easily, the trainees will find feeding tables very convenient. Have one at hand with a doll seated in it. These tables allow comfortable and safe feeding of baby and plenty of surface for spills or exploratory feels or pokes at food. Food that tastes good often feels good, and vice versa! Several feeding tables may be placed together. Can the trainees tell you why this is a good idea? Aside from convenience to the feeding person, the trainees may point out the pleasant, sociable time that meals provide. Babies that eat together in small groups of three or four may become interested in foods they see another trying, but which they formerly refused. Ask the trainees how

they would go about introducing a new meat or vegetable. Agree heartily when they suggest offering small portions, not pressuring infants to eat more than they are comfortable with, or offering a bit of new food along with a preferred familiar food.

Meal times are a good time to teach babies eating motions and noises. Lip-smacking or mouth-opening by baby can be imitated with a grin by his caregiver. A baby's pleasurable recognition of his own gesture and his further performance of his eating motions enhances his zest for food. As he eats, the caregiver nods approval, smiles, and says, "Mm, carrots. Good carrots for Darrell." Ask the trainees to pretend to feed the dolls seated in feeding tables or to feed each other. If a trainee is role-playing the baby, ask her to refuse food by turning away her head or pursing her lips. Make sure the trainees do not force food on a baby. Of course, if an adult waits a bit, a baby who perhaps just needed more time to keep a spoonful of food in his mouth and to swallow it, may be ready for more food despite his initial refusal. Meal times should be relaxed and pleasant, not rushed

THE ADULT-CHILD FEEDING PROCESS SHOULD HELP THE INFANT TO BUILD FEELINGS OF SECURITY AND TRUST IN OTHERS.

or anxious despite a baby's possibly finicky appetite. Remember that eating, in the mind of the infant, is linked closely to mothering.

Finger Foods

For the older baby who is learning to eat finger foods, it is important to provide an assortment of colors and tastes that are convenient for a baby to handle, and safe for him to eat. Ask the trainees if they can choose from the following list which would be appropriate (starred) foods for a year-old baby, and which are not yet appropriate to set out.

> grated raw apple*
>
> cubes of cooked liver
>
> cubes of raw apple
>
> crumbled yellow cheese*
>
> carrot sticks
>
> Rice Krispies*
>
> cooked tiny green peas*

chopped cooked egg*

soft thin slivers of cooked ham*

whole raisins

cooked round thin slices of carrot*

whole grapes

shredded cooked chicken*

small rounds of skinless hot dogs*

soft, cooked strands of spaghetti*

<u>Dinner Done: Fuss Or Fun?</u>

Talk with the trainees about how to end meal times gracefully.
Sometimes babies can be very messy or sleepy, or both. The
finish of a feeding session should not be a tension-producing

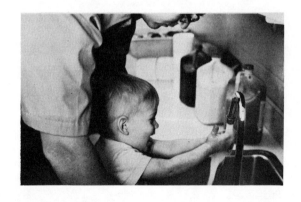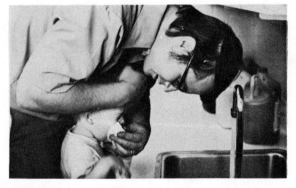

experience for the baby. If a caregiver tries to shove into
his mouth an unwanted "last spoonful," feeding times may end
in a fight-to-the-finish (or to a draw) as baby spits out the
unwelcome portion! Washup is part of food time. Saying, "Time
to wash up now," as one goes over to the sink for a washcloth
helps a baby prepare for the washcloth you are bringing. Gently

talking about washing faces and washing hands as the baby is
cleaned may entertain him enough so he doesn't fuss or squirm
away. A small pan of clean water brought to the table for
baby to swish hands through makes the cleanup period less
difficult for a baby who becomes quite irritable at this time.
Talking in a soothing voice to a sleepy baby who wants only
his bed after a bottle or meal makes a necessary diaper change
go easier before that nap.

What Baby Learns With Feeding

Food variety not only entices the eye and the palate, but
challenges little fingers to adapt to sizes and shapes varying
from a wiggly spaghetti strand to a slippery round cooked
carrot slice. Learning to manage a training cup or a spoon
is also a large job for a baby. So feeding time is a
learning time too. Be sure that the trainees, as they
summarize what a baby learns from his feeding experiences, have
absorbed the essentials.

> The caregiver is a reliable provider of stomach comfort,
> sucking comfort, and help, if needed, by a baby who
> finds feeding himself still a very hard chore.

> Since it is the baby who gets the caregiver "to give"
> food to him, he develops feelings of competence.
> Learning that he can get someone to feed him when he
> is hungry is an important early experience for an
> infant. Later on, the baby to whom adults have given
> food generously and when he has needed it will more
> easily be able "to give" himself. An older baby often
> "feeds" a loved caregiver a morsel of his food. He
> wants his caregiver to see and taste things he enjoys
> seeing and tasting, to share in the interesting
> experiences of his life. The adult who feeds a baby

well also feeds the wellsprings of his ability to give to others.

Baby has a right to choose the tempo of his feeding, whether with milk or solids, as well as the substance: Assortments of size, color, texture increase his chances to learn that he is competent and can make good choices for himself.

New taste and food texture experiences can be positive.

Eating is a <u>sociable</u> occasion.

Finger-pickup skills increase as baby adapts to assorted sizes and shapes of food.

Spills and dribbling and squeezing samples of foods are natural pathways to learning to eat in a more grownup fashion. The caregiver should accept that baby sometimes goes on binges of special food likes and dislikes.

The caregiver who can be trusted to satisfy in a pleasant and adventuresome manner baby's important and basic feeding needs, can be more easily accepted by him as the teacher of new and difficult social and physical skills. A trusting relation carries over to things other than feeding, and she may find that she can encourage a baby to persist at tasks or efforts which are new or hard for him after she has satisfied his feeding needs.

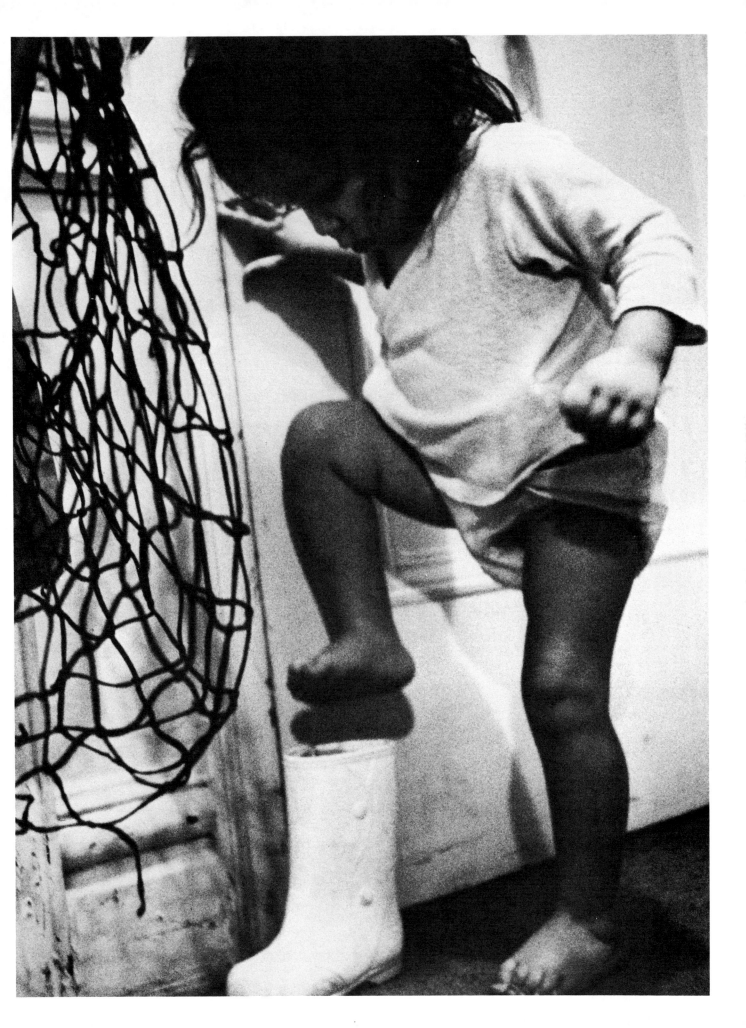

3

LARGE-MUSCLE SKILLS

Gross Motor Development: Planning

In preparation for these sessions:

■——➤Invite mothers and infants of assorted ages to participate
in this session.

■——➤Show the trainees some of the figures and tables which
illustrate different creeping styles, or age ranges within
which most babies usually accomplish a given motor skill.*

■——➤If you can, rent films from the Gesell Institute in New
Haven, Connecticut. These will give the trainees a
clearer picture of how a motor skill grows from its
initial appearance, through consolidation and increasing
effectiveness of the new skill, to its coordination with
other motor skills. For example, the newly standing,
still wobbly, year old baby cannot combine standing alone
and bending the torso in order to pick up a bit of
cracker fallen from his fingers. Once he has practiced
and further perfected his recently-acquired skills, he
will attempt such combinations with plenty of toppling
at first as he tries.

Description Of Motor Skill Development

Start your explorations into motor development by getting the

trainees to name many early actions of a baby which involve

large muscles. They should name such gross motor actions as

leg kicking or lifting a chin off a mat when placed in prone

position (on his stomach). If they have seen the Caldwell

film, *How Babies Learn*, trainees may also mention the fact

that "mass" or total body action rather than specific movement

{ *Mussen, Conger and Kagan, Chapter 5, "Biological Changes in }
the First Year."

responses of arms and legs are common in a very young baby. They should also mention that mastery over newly-emerging gross motor skills may be very inadequate to the baby's expressed needs. An infant may express an animated desire to grasp the attractive toy just ahead of him out of reach, but his initial creeping efforts may thrust him backwards away from the toy! Tell the trainees about kinds of orphanage experiences.* Babies left on their backs on soft mattresses for long periods in a monotonous environment showed a marked delay in developing large-muscle skills.

Then, for contrast, describe the study by McGraw of the twins, Johnny and Jimmy. McGraw used a carefully-sequenced training program and was able to teach one of the twins roller skating and other large-muscle skills when he was very young.

Body Games: A Physical And Psychological Boost For Baby

Talk to the trainees about how a caregiver helps a young baby enjoy the feel of stretches and flexions of his own body. Stretch and then flex your own arms and legs and torso to demonstrate these actions for the trainees. Make sure that the trainees understand that not only does a caregiver do body exercises with a baby, but she continuously encourages a baby's self-initiated efforts to attain new skills and competences with his own muscles. Babies who try out new physical skills

{ *Dennis and Najarian. }

43

with such adult encouragement are being given an important psychological boost by a caregiver. A sense of mastery over one's own musculature, direction of movement and body functions produces an assured baby. He knows he can manage himself -- why not the whole world!

Physical exercises for young babies and older children also provide a sociable occasion for chuckles and laughter and a special togetherness for caregiver and infant. An adult and child who throw a bean bag or roll a ball back and forth between them create a special feeling of friendliness for each other. Action games played with a baby provide him with some of his earliest social activities.

Body Games With Babies

For the rest of these sessions on gross motor skills you and the trainees will carry out physical exercises and large-muscle games with infants. As you carry out exercises with a guest baby point out to the trainees what part of the baby's body gets a chance to stretch or flex in this body game. Demonstrate how to move limbs gently, not jerkily or suddenly. Point out how the baby's responses to the games are giving you clues whether you can do a game once or several times. Even a simple exercise like lifting baby to standing position while holding his fingers may frighten a baby who is unsure of his ability to stand. Show the trainees ways you (or the mother if she is present) modify your game yet accomplish the same exercise for a baby who is just beginning to gain control over his muscles. For example, the caregiver can kneel down and hug baby around the waist, for firm support, with baby's arms leaning on her shoulder or around her neck. With this extra physical security and closeness, an unsure baby may be willing to try some moments of standing. If your earrings are glittery and dangling, baby may even "forget" his fears for a few minutes as he stands and reaches to explore the earrings.

The following instructions for 13 body games* are written so that you can read them rapidly while showing the trainees how to do them. You can also read them out loud to a trainee as she practices doing a body game with a guest infant <u>after</u> you have demonstrated the game for her.

Arm Stretch

While your baby is on a flat padded surface, such as a feeding table or a floor rug, hold both his hands in yours and stretch his arms gently out. Then curl them in and wrap them in a hug about his own body with a little shake. Smile and talk to baby. Vocalize "out again" and "in again" or other appropriate

*See if the trainees can tell you which games are appropriate for very young infants, which for older infants, and which games can be enjoyed by both older and younger infants.

rhythmic words as you repeat bringing the arms out and then in.
[1.]

Hold baby's hands as in the first arm exercise. Bring them gently in a wide arc along the surface or in the air until they are above his head. Then bring the arms down at his sides. A chant such as "up we go...and...down again" with a smile contributes to the pleasurable body feeling of the stretch.
[2.]

Leg: Flex And Stretch

While the baby is on a chang-ing table or a floor, take his legs in your hands and bend them gently so the knees come close to the stomach. Then stretch the legs down again. Chant, "Bend your knees and stre-etch your legs," or some such words in rhythm to the motions you are doing. The baby will enjoy a mild "tickle" with his own knees if you jiggle

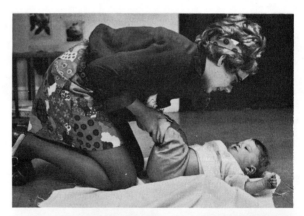

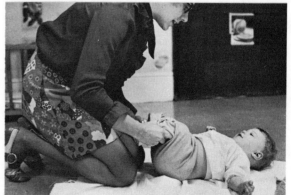

them on his stomach occasionally as you bend them. Smile and
look in his eyes directly as you play with him. Then play the
game with each leg separately. [3.]

Leg Kicks

With baby either safely buckled on a changing table, or lying
on his back in a play pen, attach an interesting mobile with
sturdy toys, such as nursery birds, over the vicinity of his
feet. Adjust the height so that the mobile toys will be set
in motion easily by a kick. Swing the toys in the air once or
twice to attract his attention and to arouse his body motions.
If the infant doesn't, by an accidental kick, set the mobile
toys in motion after staring at them a while, swing one of his
legs so it kicks the mobile. Let him watch the result. Urge
him to "go get the toys" with his feet. Some 4 month olds
can enjoy this exercise for almost 20 minutes. [4.]

Kick a large ball with your foot. Say "Kick the ball, Barry,
kick the ball." Smile and say, "That's it, kick the ball,"
at any kind of initial body contact the infant makes with the
ball. If he does not push the ball with a leg at all in
imitation of you, steady his body with your arm and help his
leg to kick the ball. As you do this, say, "Barry, kick the
ball." [5.]

Torso: Flex And Stretch

Place baby on his stomach on a floor, and get him to lift his chin off the ground by snapping your fingers so he looks up at the source of the sound. Keep one hand flat on his chest and move his legs up in the air with your other hand, so only his torso is touching the surface. Rock him gently, as a boat on a wave. Chant, "Rock, rock, rock; Darryl is rocking." [6.]

Curl your baby up in a ball on a floor rug so his head and toes touch over his stomach. Tickle his hair gently with his toes. This may also be done conveniently with baby lying on one side. [7.]

Hold baby firmly by his middle. Now lift him above your head toward an interesting mobile or wall decoration. Urge him several times to reach for or "to get" the toy. Allow baby  to touch or swipe at the object toward which he is stretching. Finish the game with a shake to his tummy and a hug, and exclamations of pleasure at his efforts as you lower him into your arms and then down to a play area. A variant of this exercise is to hold the baby up in the air and swoop him down-ward on an incline toward the floor.

Hold him firmly. If he stretches his body and arms, he should be able to reach an attractive toy you have placed on the floor. [8.]

Sit comfortably with a baby under 8 months sitting on your
knees facing you. Clasp your arms behind him supporting his
back and neck, and rock back and forth as far in each direction
as is comfortable or enjoyable. Chant a "see-saw" song for him.

Sit an older infant on your lap,
with one leg hanging down from
either side of your lap. Clasp
hands and see-saw similarly with
him. Increase the amount of the
rocking motion as the baby grows
more accustomed to the game and

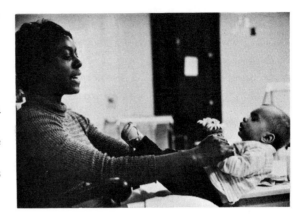

enjoys the increased bending of his torso from a deep back bend
to a far forward bend. With an older baby, this game may be
played on the floor: Sit facing the infant. Form a V around
the baby with your legs. Then play a "see-saw" game. Chanting
"Whee! down we go, and up," as baby moves from the leaning over
backwards to the sit up position adds rhythm and pleasure to
the exercise. You may also vary this game by swaying from left
to right with the infant in this sitting position. [9.]

Lay a baby on a rug or floor mat. An infant who is particularly
inactive and who cannot get about on his own may need a lot of
loving play-talk in order to enjoy this roll-over-on-side-and-
roll-back-again game. Rolling may begin with baby on his back
(supine) or on his stomach (in a prone position). An active
infant may be stimulated to roll his body without physical
help from a caregiver. If she can make interesting and funny

vocal or toy sounds on either side of him, baby will roll over to see the source of the funny noise. [10.]

Torso Bends With Pick Ups

Drop interesting toys (a red ball or a striped plastic candy cane, for example) in front of the toddling infant. Point to each toy as it is dropped in turn and say, "Danny, pick up the ball." "Go get it!" Clap for the child if he bends and picks up the toy. This is a good game for coordinating large-muscle and fine pick-up skills. If the baby drops to the floor for a pick up, let him; then help him learn an easier way to pick up the toy. Lift him to his feet and show him yourself how to bend down from a standing position to pick up objects. Steady him with your arms so that he can imitate you in bending over to pick up a toy. If baby is good at bending to pick up toys, then show him how to squat and pick up toys. Let him squat to pick up a toy. Act proud of his actions even if he is only partially successful. [11.]

Social Rhythm Games

Some exercises have a strong component of social play in them. They not only help the baby's body to enjoy rhythm and to grow strong and capable, they also teach him that such sports can be particularly enjoyable with other people -- both adults and children.

Demonstrate for trainees by role-playing the games with babies, or have visiting mothers try out these games with their infants.

Then ask the trainees to try these games with babies. Ask them to watch their babies for signs of interest or tuning out. Encourage the trainees to vary their rhythms for the dance game. For example, they may want to try out a short-long rhythm. Ask other trainees to comment out loud what else besides beating rhythms the demonstrating trainee has to do to encourage a baby to bounce or dance. Trainees should notice the importance of an adult's smiles, head bobbing and torso bending as she invites babies to rhythmicize.

Torso Bounce And Dancing

This game can become an early kind of dance party for babies. Get together a group of infants (9 to 10 months and older); they may be standing freely or seated in infant sling seats. Have the trainer demonstrate how to beat out or play simple rhythms on a drum or tambourine or a wastebasket turned upside down. Long-short beats are helpful for getting a baby to bounce his buttocks to rhythm. Tap your feet and lean your own body forward as you chant, "Boom-boom, boom-boom, boom-boom, boom!" *Mary had a little lamb, Row, row, row your boat* or *Frere Jacques* are good songs in this rhythm to accompany your drum beat. "Dancey, dancey, dancey, dance," chanted as you sway and beat out the rhythm, works well too. Infants also enjoy long-short-short rhythms, as in the nursery rhyme, *Hickory, dickory, dock, the mouse ran up the clock*, which also contains short-long rhythms. [12.]

Riding Horse Rhythms

Sit comfortably with an infant seated on your knees facing you. The infant should be able to sit well without support before you try this game. Chant, "This is the way the farmer rides," two times; "Giddy-yap, giddy-yap," two times. Move your knees so that the child is rocked in a slow, bobbing motion. Next, chant, "This is the way the trotter rides," two times; "O trot, O trot, O trot, O trot," and bounce the child in a quicker riding-horse fashion on your knees. Finally, chant, "This is the way my pony rides," two times, "Gallup, gallup, gallup, gallup!" Accent the second syllable of "GalLUP." Vigorously and rapidly pitch the child in a rocking-horse motion on your knees. End the game by drawing the child to you in a joyous hug. He may ask to play the riding-horse game again. Be sure to start the game over with very slow motions at first. When playing with an older baby who has learned the word *more*, ask, "Johnny, want to play *more* riding horse? When the baby has become familiar with this game, he may initiate slower and faster buttock movements to each phase of the ride as soon as he hears the words and rhythmic speed of the chant. [13.]

The Inactive Baby: Do's And Dont's

Now that you and the trainees have a variety of motion games and exercises for baby, this is a good time to ask the trainees how they would encourage a baby who has a low level of physical activity and tends mostly to stay put on his stomach (prone position), or back (supine position). Praise trainees if they suggest that the adult must first watch for any signs of motion. If that baby waves an arm, flexes his body or kicks a leg, the caregiver can coo, or sing a few notes to him, or give him a clean finger to suck on briefly, or rub his back or stomach gently. Do the trainees remember that we call these special attentions a caregiver dispenses right after a baby does any actions she is trying to encourage "positive reinforcers?" How would the trainees encourage creeping in a year-old sedentary baby? They may, if they wish, demonstrate for you with a visiting infant. One method you may suggest is to wiggle an interesting pull-toy (or toys attached to yarns or strings) close to an infant's hand. As he starts to creep, the toy is moved a bit away from him. Baby is allowed to reach and play with the toy after any sign of vigorous limb motions. All his efforts at moving from one place to another are praised.

Readiness For Learning Motor Skills

One infant may walk at 8 to 10 months, a second baby may not walk until 16 months or even slightly later. We do not try to "walk" the second baby around the room by holding his hands while his feet drag and he cries unhappily. We do continue to play body games with him; we do tempt him to creep for toys on wheels or for bright strings which are a bit beyond his reach; we do dangle a well-liked toy above or beside or in back of him, so that the seated baby stretches upward or outward or swivels on his behind in order to reach for the toy. We nod encouragement, clap for him and praise him for trying to get the toy, and we let him get the toy if he stretches somewhat for it. We do provide a variety of furniture such as couches, low sturdy tables, etc., on which the baby can pull himself to standing, or can begin to take steps while supporting himself with his arms. Such furniture (which may even be doll-corner, child-size stoves and cupboards) should have handles, knobs or armrests to provide supports for the unsteady walker.

BE SURE THE TRAINEES UNDERSTAND THAT NOT ALL BABIES ARE READY TO LEARN THE SAME LARGE-MUSCLE SKILLS AT THE SAME TIME.

Ask the trainees questions to bring out their understanding of the progression of locomotion. Babies who are still wary of standing alone are not ready to trot around a room, even with support. Their crying is often a clue to this lack of readiness. We help babies to make small steps forward in their skills. When a baby has had a chance to practice a prior skill for walking, namely, standing securely alone with support, then he will be ready to try the next step which will be his first step! The trainees should now be able to suggest more

DO NOT FORCE NEW BEHAVIORS WHEN THE NECESSARY PRIOR SKILLS ARE LACKING.

modest measures, such as this learning-to-walk game to
encourage that first step:

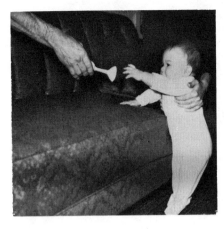 Wiggle or ride an attractive toy on a
couch slowly away from a standing baby
clutching the couch, so that at least
a step or two is necessary before the
baby can reach the toy. Urge, "Johnny,
get the toy!" If the baby succeeds in
taking a step with support, praise him
and say, "Johnny's walking." If he falls on the floor, move
the toy back to his end of the couch so that if he pulls
himself to standing, he will be able to reach the toy. Say,
"Here's the doggie, bow-wow-wow," or "Here comes the car,
zoom, zoom, zoom," as you move the toy within his reach. Once
he has handled and enjoyed the toy, again move it out of reach.
After two unsuccessful attempts, push the toy near the baby so
he can get it without a step. Try a day or two later to see
if he is more ready at that time to take his first steps.

Equipment To Advance Motor Skills

The walking, climbing toddler needs lots of practice to perfect
his newly-acquired motoric expertise. If you have already
ordered stairs for climbing and jumping, rocking boats, slides
and trikes, show this equipment to the trainees. As they walk
around and look at each piece of equipment, have the trainees

tell you what special skill-sharpening help each piece of
equipment may provide. If these Center playthings are not yet
available, show catalogue illustrations of them to the trainees.
Ask them questions so they explain to you the special potential
of each piece of equipment for aiding large-muscle development.

4

PICK-UP AND HANDLING SKILLS

<u>The Goals For Trainees</u>

The extraordinary changes in an infant's ability to pick up and
handle objects in the first years of life will be the initial
focus of your sessions on manipulation skills. These
manipulation skills include many different infant finger and
hand activities such as a young baby's struggle to feed himself
a spoonful of cereal from his bowl, his efforts to pull mommy's
bracelet onto his own wrist, his fitting puzzle pieces
together, or his pouring water from a pot into a cup without
spilling much. The second phase of study will be the ways in
which toddlers increase their handling skills. A workshop in
which the trainees make toys to help an infant's manipulation
skills as well as familiarization of trainees with commercially
prepared materials, such as puzzles and pegboards, will be the
third goal of training sessions in fine-motor coordination.*

*Teaching trainees and demonstrating for them manipulative
games and tasks appropriate for infants: Parker, Provence
and Huntington, pp. 175-183 and Appendix C, and the John
Tracy Clinic materials.
  Specific instructions for manipulation games with older
toddlers, with emphasis on labeling of motions and on
presentation of tasks in increasing order of their
difficulty: Palmer, F., Appendix E, Instructor's Manual.
  Instructions for making items: Schaefer and Aronson,
*Infant Education Research Project: Unpolished Curriculum
Work Papers*; Segner and Patterson, *Ways to Help Babies
Grow and Learn*; Gordon and Lally's *Intellectual Stimulation
for Infants and Toddlers*.

Despite many descriptions of specific small-muscle tasks and handling games, make clear to the trainees that we are not interested particularly in training an ability, for example, to build a four-block tower a month earlier than most babies can! We *are* trying to create a *climate for exploration* of toys and materials by the babies. We are trying to provide a rich variety of toys which are appropriate for each different ability level a baby reaches. This way an infant can try out new ways of handling toys no matter how recently developed or how advanced are his fine-motor skills.

The trainee best helps the baby when she arranges his experiences so he can help himself increase his own competence in handling objects. A six month old may still have trouble getting his hand to reach out for bright cradle-gym toys suspended over his crib. A caregiver can slip over the infant's hand a bright red glove made of soft stretchable cotton or orlon. If she has cut the fingertips off this glove, baby's fingertips will stick through the glove. His hand is much more vivid to look at now. As a result he may find it easier to keep track of his hand *and* an object he is trying to reach. Now he can practice reaching and grasping skills on his own. He has had an assist from the caregiver who sized up his fine-motor skill problems in one area, and helped make them less frustrating for him.

Demonstration and discussion of the development of infant
manipulation skills will have much more impact with real infant
models. If this is not possible, prepare a video-tape in advance
to demonstrate the development of finger and hand skills, and
eye-hand coordinations. Include baby-modeled sequences of both
initial and consolidated stages in the development of such skills.
The "initial stage" of a skill often is described by parents or
caregivers as "clumsy handling." A baby somehow gathers up and

clutches a lima bean in his whole hand.
It is hard for him to push the bean through
a one-inch diameter hole or slot cut in a
jar top. His own hand gets in the way.
The bean may slither along the jar lid
and baby's efforts to poke it or shove
it into the hole may not succeed. Contrast
this early or initial stage of his skill
with "consolidated" skills he may show in this game at around
15 months. Then he may quickly and precisely swoop down on the
lima bean from above, using only his thumb and forefinger, carry
the bean up with assurance and plunk it with satisfaction through
the small jar-top hole. Include in your video-tape situations
in which an infant is presented with an unbreakable cup; one,
two or more blocks; balls of aluminum foil in sizes of less than
1" diameter; metal, plastic and wooden basting spoons; shoe
laces; ponytail yarns; ring stack sets; rattles; hammering

pegboards; and xylophones. Focus the camera on the different
reaching and grasping methods used by infants of different
ages for obtaining and exploring objects of varying sizes and
shapes. Vary the distance from the baby at which objects are
presented, from quite near the hand to several inches away.
Present items on the side of the reaching hand, at the body
midline, and on the side opposite the reaching hand to
illustrate:

➤ Differential capacities of young infants to deal with
   objects at such locations,

➤ infant persistence in efforts to obtain objects,

➤ the development of one-handedness, as well as the
   special functions of each hand either for holding
   or for operating on objects such as the hammering
   pegboard.

The video-tape does not necessarily need to be made with
progressively older or more competent babies modeling each
sequence. You may video-tape infant models in scrambled
order of skill development. You can show such a developmentally-
scrambled sequence to the trainees when you have finished your
discussions on fine-motor skills. Ask them to decide which
infants have more developed manipulation skills. Trainees will
have to make decisions despite your scrambled sequencing, or
despite the fact that an older-looking infant in the video-tape
may show only rudimentary accomplishments in manipulatory skills
compared to a younger, but more advanced, infant. If you stage

such contrasting models in your video-tape, you will be able to
make more vivid the point that enhancement of fine pick-ups and
handling skills (just as with large-muscle skills, such as
crawling or walking) depends not only on a baby's growing
abilities with increasing age, but also on relevant opportunities
and encouragement for his motor learning.

Modeling With Small-Muscle Toys

If no demonstration films or infants are available, the trainees
will still be able to understand the various stages of infant
grasping and handling* *if you model infant grasping and handling
for them and get them to model back to you.*

You will need in advance to gather an assortment of commercially-
available, as well as home-found, toys and games which encourage
small-muscle manipulations and eye-hand coordinations. Use these
toys, games and materials for your modeling demonstrations.
The table of small-muscle toys and the table of home-found
handling toys which follow list a variety of appropriate items.

Pick-Ups: A Discussion Of The Development Of Small-Muscle Skills

Ask the trainees how a baby first picks up interesting objects in
his surroundings. If the trainees seem puzzled, give them a hint
by asking how a baby picks out interesting people. The eyes are

{ *Mussen, Conger and Kagan, p. 172, p. 178. }

the first tool babies use to "pick up"
and pick out familiar or new sights
and spectacles in their world. Only
toward the middle of the first year
do babies reach and grasp with hands
for rattles and colorful toys which
caregivers offer so enticingly to them.
Of course, the reflex grasp of infants
younger than four months enables them

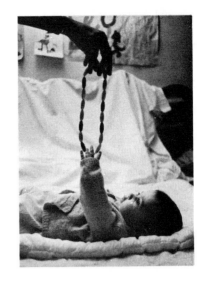

to clutch objects -- whether toys or long hair -- which their
hands happen to touch. Wiggle your index fingers into the
curled fists of a very young baby and he can hold on very tightly,
with enough force so that you can gently raise him from his back
to a sit-up position. But deliberate and intentional pick-ups
of objects can only occur as the baby's reaching and voluntary
grasping skills grow and are practiced.

Place one of your guest babies, younger than six months, in an
infant seat, or let his mother cradle him so that he is
comfortably propped with his back against her stomach. He should
be able to reach a toy on the tabletop in front of him. Dangle
an interesting and colorful toy in front of the baby. Ask the
trainees to describe how the baby is responding. His eyes
rivet on the toy. Often his arms rise up and his hands and
maybe legs move vigorously in response to the spectacle of a
dangled or moving toy. He may begin to reach outward or upward
toward toys. In the beginning his hands may swipe at the toys.

Only gradually will he become able to seize them victoriously. Ask your trainees if they were busy with three other infants in their care how might they arrange good practice experiences for a fourth baby who is just learning to coordinate his swipes and grasps. They will probably be able to suggest the use of rattles, plastic rings and safe, sturdy, easily-cleanable toys on elastic strings suspended over cribs, playpens or carriages so that the toys can swing freely close at hand for baby to set in motion or clasp.

A six-month-old baby may have already succeeded in grasping large objects such as blocks, or managed to lift a plastic cup by its handle from a tabletop in front of him. Now you or a trainee can present small objects, such as bits of cold breakfast cereal or the colorful red cinnamon drops used to decorate cakes. Again, encourage the trainees to call out and comment on what is happening. Make sure they describe the raking motion by which primarily the middle fingers of the infant's hand are working to pick up a toy. Do trainees note the persistence of these raking motions of the hand as an infant at about this age tries and tries again to pick up a tiny toy? You may model the "rake" yourself. Demonstrate the frustrations of this early pick-up method. Often the baby who uses the rake motion flips a tiny toy further away from his eager reach. If there are older infants present (such as a 9 month and a 12-13 month old), have them seated also on trainees' (or mothers') laps, so that they are close to the table tops. Ask the trainees to comment on what happens when they present older babies with large toys such as blocks, compared to smaller objects, such as pieces of cold cereal and cinnamon drops. Make sure the trainees have noted well the progression of hand manipulation skills from the earliest swipes and <u>raking motions</u>, through the <u>scissors motions</u>, where the whole hand is still much involved in pick-ups despite the

increasing usefulness of thumb and index finger, all the way to the triumphant efficiency of the <u>pincer</u> pick-up. With the pincer grasp baby can pick up with only his thumb or forefinger even such odd-shaped tiny objects as bread crumbs or dust from under the living room couch! The trainees should remark on how much more smoothly the older infant seems to be able to reach directly for what he sees. The older baby opens and shapes his hand <u>before</u> it gets to the object in order to be better able to grasp that particular size and shape item. Young babies reach with both hands for toys. Older babies seem to have one hand in advance, and later on, reach with a single hand more often, though they may not exhibit strong preference for which hand that is. Ask the trainees to call out all the actions that babies up to a year and a half seem to be doing with toys. In their catalogue should be various reaches and grasps, bringing to mouth, waving or shaking, banging, pulling, pushing, poking with index finger, turning objects around in hand, banging objects together, holding more than one object in each hand, putting one object inside another or taking an object out of a container.

Some of the demonstrating babies may be able to hold on to two objects but never spontaneously combine them together. Others may attempt to bang two toys together, especially if you or a trainee models this action for the infant. But the two toys may

POINT OUT TO THE TRAINEES HOW GRADUALLY SOME OF THESE ACTIONS AND SKILLS ARE PERFECTED.

slide against one another, or even miss contact completely as the two arms pass each other in the banging-together motion. Which toys seem easier for babies to bang together? Make sure the trainees notice that babies need to be offered items in a large variety of sizes and shapes and textures and weights, to practice manipulations, but some toys are easier in the early stages of practice than others. Ask the trainees to guess whether a ten-month-old baby would find a pair of light plastic cups, or a pair of long thin wooden basting spoons, easier to bang or click together. Plastic cups are easier because of their shape, weight and ease in handling.

If none of the trainees has mentioned hand releases as yet, either get a baby to demonstrate, or model yourself the sequences of learning to release objects from a grasp. Babies often drop objects or throw them. Putting objects down deliberately and gently takes a certain level of development and lots of practice in "letting go." The trainees may be surprised after you have modeled "in the cup" (releasing a block from your hand into a cup) with a block for an 11 month old. You have urged him with smiles to imitate you and put this toy inside a large container. Yet the infant hand which has just compliantly descended into the cup clutching a toy comes back up out of the cup still clutching the same toy.

Ability to control the angle at which a toy is held is another skill which requires lots of practice. Ask the trainees to offer babies just over a year crayons or pegs and pegboards. Get them to notice the kinds of troubles babies may have in adjusting the angle of holding a crayon so that it can leave a mark on a paper. Similarly, if the angle of holding a peg is too acute, the peg will slide in a frustrating way all around the peg hole without ever settling in. Model for the trainee how a small assist to a baby hand can tilt it more effectively so he can get his peg into a hole. What kinds of games can the trainees think of which can help babies improve wrist and finger control? They should be able now to suggest soft finger foods which will help boost pick up and release skills.

Give babies plastic basins with water to scoop into and pour from orange juice cans, cups or pots.

Give babies egg cartons with an egg-shaped dot of color painted at the bottom of each cup. Encourage the baby to use his <u>forefinger</u> to touch the dot or point to the dot in each cup.

Sing a song to the babies (using a tune like *All Around The Mulberry Bush*) as you rotate your wrists. Put a finger puppet on one finger of each hand. You might try words like, "This is the way our puppets turn, puppets turn, puppets turn. This is the way our puppets turn, and then fall down!" As you sing "fall down," turn your wrists downward so the finger puppet heads flop downward. Thus, you model for the babies a side-to-side wrist motion and a down-up wrist motion as you turn your wrists down and then upward for the game to begin.

Lift babies up to light switches or chain pulls, and let them flip a switch on and off, or pull a chain to light a lamp. Label the motions and praise the baby's effort. That much "push" or "pull" may be strenuous work for tiny hands.

Wriggle shoe laces, ponytail yarns or thin strips of cloth on a table top. Model for the baby how to pinch the thin material between thumb or forefinger in order to grasp it. Smile and praise him for his "pick-ups."

Give baby a closed plastic shaker (tall plastic salt shakers may be used) with red beans or colored macaroni. These shakers can be made during the materials creation session which will follow your modeling-teaching session. As the baby tilts the shaker, the beans will pour to one side or another. He will begin to associate the weight feeling in his wrist with his handling of the shaker and seeing the beans massed at one end of the shaker or the other.

Complicated Manipulations:
How Trainees Can Gain Rapport With Guest Babies

Older children in the second and third year of life may now serve as demonstrators of more advanced manipulations. These babies may prefer to sit on mother's lap as the younger ones did; or they may feel comfortable on a rug, sitting in and among the trainees on the floor. Provide toys such as: Boxes and drawers to reach into and pull things out of; musical instruments; hammering toys; assorted puzzles of graded difficulty; stacking toys; pop-it beads. The toys that the trainees offer the infants and demonstrate for them should include both those with which each baby can succeed comfortably, and those where the required skills still need adult help or further practice or task simplification.

If the toddlers are shy, model yourself, or ask the trainees to model some tasks while conversing gently and interesting the babies in the materials to put them at ease. Pull two large plastic bangle bracelets onto your wrist. Talk to the babies about your putting a bracelet on or taking it off as you do so. After you take one bracelet off, ask the baby if he can take the other off your wrist. Put one on baby's wrist and smile happily, saying, "Bracelet on Terry!" Let a baby pull the bracelet off or put it on you or himself. These simple, personal games with toddlers focus on materials and actions. They serve to introduce babies to, and make them feel more comfortable with, new people.

A music box that is set in motion by turning a knob, or a
plastic pinwheel that is set in motion by blowing air on it
are interesting toys which produce attractive auditory (hear-
able) or visual (see-able) experiences which can absorb a
toddler's interest so he loses his reluctance to interact
with the trainee "strangers" or their toys.

Incentives Or Rewards

Incentives are special rewards which make us work harder to
get them. We learn more easily when the rewards of our work
are very attractive or important to us. Talk with the trainee
about all the kinds of rewards babies enjoy. Just as babies
differ in the strength of their basic needs, so do they
respond differently to different kinds and amounts of urging
or praise or attention to help them learn fine-motor skills or
carry out simple tasks. Ask the trainees for stories about
babies they may have known who didn't respond very much to one
or another kind of reward or incentive. A baby indifferent to
verbal praise alone may brighten up and strive even harder,
for example, to adjust a large piece on a puzzle-board if a
caregiver leans forward with a *cheek caress and a kiss* while
saying, "Good for you. You got it in!" Some trainees may
volunteer examples of babies who squirm out of a hug or pat.
But that baby might look up expectantly for his caregiver's
appreciative *nod and smile* when he has completed a game of
nesting containers. Another toddler praises and claps for

himself elaborately at every small step of his task. He may love the caregiver's positive *agreement*, "Yes you did it yourself!," with his triumphant assertion, "I doo'ed it, I doo'ed it myself!"

Some babies need *reassurance and cheering on* at every step of a game, where, for example, Montessori cylinders are to be placed in their matching holes. Another toddler may look at an adult from under lowered lids until he is sure the adult has withdrawn her attention. When the adult looks absorbed in her work, then that baby may competently and fairly quickly replace all the pegs in a Wallin pegboard. Only then will he accept, with a shy smile, the caregiver's *admiring comments*.

Some babies find some toys more rewarding than others. The toys may be easier to handle or have brighter colors, or maybe jingling sounds, or taste better. A caregiver might urge a 14-month-old baby to accept

71

and hold a third toy in his hands without dropping the other two he already has. If the toys she holds out to him successively are ones he prefers, then he may try harder to hold them all. When a caregiver stages a new kind of learning experience for a baby, she should try to use toys a baby finds rewarding to try to get. Thus, if a caregiver wants to give an 8-month-old baby a chance to practice pulling a toy to himself by means of an attached string, she might start with a thick, short string (which is easy to grasp and pull), and tie it to a rattle which the baby particularly enjoys.

Some toddlers work much more cheerfully at a color or shape matching game if they find a bit of food (a snip of miniature marshmallow, perhaps) under the correct match. Incentive or reward conditions may change drastically with age. The trainees may be amused to consider what their own most valuable incentive conditions are. But approval and tangible rewards in some form will encourage learning efforts at almost any stage. Sensitivity to each infant's preferred incentives helps the caregiver nurture each infant's learning career optimally.

Holding And Operating

Ask your trainees to watch how older babies use each hand for more specialized work. Be sure they notice, for example, that a toddler needs to hold his paper with one hand so it

doesn't slip from under his
grasp while he scribbles with a
Magic Marker or crayon or piece
of chalk clutched in his other
hand. Caregivers who are alert
to such slipping mishaps and the
different uses of each hand can

help a baby better to steady his materials with one hand as he
works or operates on them with the other hand. Ask the trainees
what other toys that you have set out require these seaprate
holding and acting-on efforts for each hand. They should
mention that most toys made up of more than one part need this
double action.

Different Ways To Help

A 19 month old trying to sit a large doll in a toy chair may
find the chair and doll sliding apart from each other. Ask the
trainees to try different ways of helping each toddler to
succeed at such tasks. With some babies a light steadying
adult hand on the infant's holding hand may work best.
Pointing out to the infant that he has a free hand to steady
the chair while he sits a dolly down may work for another
infant. For the infant whose doll-sitting skills are just
emerging, the adult may find it necessary to give some
unnoticed assistance in steadying the chair or bending the doll
legs.

We cannot overemphasize the importance of praising and rewarding good work by the trainees. Some trainers have difficulty in knowing when and how to give praise. As the trainees work with infants on puzzles, Montessori cylinder placement, pegboard patterns, graduated ring stacking, fitting shapes into holes and other such games, walk around the room. Praise a trainee if you see her sustain an infant in a manipulation task against distractions of other persons or toys. Praise a trainee who waits while a toddler struggles at a task unsuccessfully (for example, to string a large wooden bead) either before she offers help or slowly and clearly models the

PREMATURE HELPFUL INTERFERENCE CAN DISCOURAGE THE INFANT JUST AS MUCH AS LACK OF SUPPORT WHEN HE NEEDS IT.

holding-operating functions of each hand in the *special sequence* of actions needed to succeed in pulling a bead onto a lace. Praise trainees who encourage a toddler to extend new limits to skills already achieved. For example, if a baby can steady a

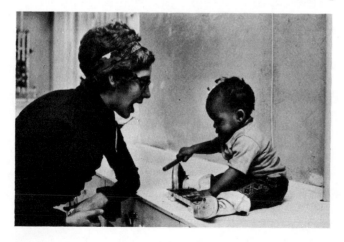

xylophone and bang haphazardly quite cheerfully and well, the trainee might demonstrate how to sound a few separate tones or ascending tones, and encourage an infant to explore new potentials of the toys and materials. A baby may

make a pop-it bead necklace and then try it on his leg, his

neck or the trainee's arm, or he may try to see if it can roll

on the floor. Praise a trainee for
modeling the action that goes with a
word she is using to urge or instruct
a baby. The trainee may want baby to
turn his puzzle piece so that the
point of a clown's conical cap fits
at the top of the head hole in a

two-piece clown puzzle. If she just says "turn the piece," or

talks about the hat pointing up, but doesn't use actions to

show what a "turn" means or where "up" or "down" are on a

puzzle board, the baby may become confused or cranky or tune

out the most patient teacher's "helpful" hints.

Consolidating Training And Sharpening Observation Skills

After you and the trainees have thanked the mothers and their

skill-modeling babies, you may want to break for coffee or to

invite the infants and mothers to lunch with the training group.

If you do lunch together, be sure to provide jars of baby food

and finger foods such as are suggested in the nutrition section.

This would be an excellent opportunity for the trainees while

eating and being sociable with the visitors to watch for infant

food preferences, refusals, self-feeding, response to maternal

feeding styles such as offering, forcing or coaxing babies.

This is a good opportunity for the trainees to practice observation skills. Which babies seem to be ready for more self-choosing of foods and more self-feeding? Are their mothers prepared to allow this independence, or do they seem to be feeding babies because of fears of messiness perhaps, or mistrust that the baby would get a balanced or sufficiently-nourishing meal if self-feeding were allowed? The trainees can also observe during lunch how mothers and babies "talk" to each other. They can become aware of a baby's babbling comments which a mother responds to or which she may ignore, thinking the baby's sounds "don't mean anything."

Toy Workshops

When the trainees have learned about small-muscle skills and demonstrated competencies in helping babies to achieve small advances and delights in such skills, it is time to hold a workshop session to construct "manipulables," toys which will provide activities and practice for infant grasping and fine-motor skills. Such workshops will also be held regularly as part of in-service training once the trainees are at work caring for infants.

Before the trainees begin their own creation of materials, make sure they have a good look at a selection of commercially-available manipulation toys. This may give them ideas which relate tasks to toy designs. They may also find ways to create some games more cheaply and simply by themselves with home-found items with which babies may be even more familiar and comfortable. They may notice a lack of commercially-available toys for certain kinds of handling or manipulation skills which they have seen babies practicing earlier.

Point to a given toy on display. Ask the trainees informally in turn what skills they think the toy will be helpful for developing. Ask other trainees to tell what skills a baby probably would need before being able to deal even on a beginning level with the requirements of a toy you are discussing. If a baby has not yet begun to use two items together, such as to clap blocks together, would it be appropriate to present to him toys which require a lot of steadying with one hand while the other hand hammers or turns a crank or plays notes? Make sure the trainees are able to tell you about many of the prior skills or coordinations which some of the more complex toys may require. On the other hand, ask them, "If a toy is too difficult for a baby to use at all, does this mean that a caregiver should never bring that toy and that baby together?" The trainees should explain to you that the baby may well enjoy, for example, watching and listening as his caregiver turns the crank on a jack-in-the-box or on a music box. Some trainees may also suggest that certain more difficult toys may be altered if a baby shows real interest, although the toy as designed is too difficult. Certain very appealing multi-piece puzzles may be modified for use by the toddler. Some of the more difficult pieces could be pasted down on the puzzle board and just a few, or even just two, more clearly identifiable pieces (a boy's hat or a car wheel, for example) could be left free for manipulation and insertion by the baby. A ring stack with many rings can be presented by a caregiver with only two of the rings available to the infant who is still struggling to place even one ring correctly. During the workshop sessions, provide as wide a selection of materials as possible for the trainees. They may prefer to work in groups of three and four or alone.

SENSITIVITY ON THE PART OF THE CAREGIVER WILL STRENGTHEN THE BABY'S FEELING THAT HE CAN ACCOMPLISH A GIVEN TASK, BECAUSE IT HAS BEEN TAILORED TO HIS SKILL LEVEL AND ATTENTION SPAN.

As you circulate among the trainees who are creating toys, ask them in non-challenging ways about the purposes and safety of toys they are making. They should be able to tell you easily how they feel that particular game or toy will enhance fine-motor skills. Some of the trainees may want your suggestions for games or toys to make.

If time and facilities are available during this workshop, home-made busyboards or wooden-wheeled pull toys may be made. Otherwise, these may be projects for later in-service training sessions. Be sure that the trainees get to see each other's productions and that each trainee has been praised for her creations in terms of their potential for increasing infant skill enjoyment and experience with manipulatory materials.

rattles

balloons

pipe cleaners

flashlights

magnets

xylophones

nesting toys

pop-it beads

ring-stack sets

busy boards*

Montessori cylinders

Play-doh, clay

pegboards, tinker toys,
pick-up sticks

large top for spinning,
twirling

large plastic jacks
that can be twirled

crayons, Magic Markers

friction vehicle toys

wind-up toys with keys to
turn; gear-turning toys

threaded plastic cylinders
which require wrist
rotations

block with varying shapes
and sizes of openings
through which matching
forms can be pushed into
the interior

soft balls with either
depression-like holes for
poking or radiating
spokes for grasping

large wooden beads in
assorted shapes, and
heavy shoe laces to
string them

household tools, plastic
screws and bolts, hammers
and pounding boards

toys which require finger
press in order to produce
a squeak; hand press toys
are also useful

toy telephones with good
dialing mechanisms

doll clothes and
furnishings; dolls

*Home-made busy boards are quite as useful and often
more appealing. They may contain a sneaker to lace,
a dinner bell, a shade-roll plus cord, a sliding
lock, a light switch which clicks up and down, a set
of gears to turn.

Empty coffee or shortening tins with slits or holes
in their plastic lids. The slits or holes, like
those in a piggy-bank, are for the insertion of
various items, such as poker chips, clean plastic
or metal bottle tops from household products, old
keys and teaspoons.

Boxes and covers of all kinds:

Empty Band-aid cans with flip-top lids.
Cardboard boxes -- rectangular candy
    boxes, round oatmeal boxes, cheese
    boxes.
Food cannisters with place-on lids that
    have a top knob for grasping; strip-
    opened orange juice cans in assorted
    nestable sizes, with place-on metal
    lids.
Clean jars with lids that can be screwed
    and unscrewed or twisted on and off.

Egg beaters with strong handles that turn easily.

Jars of different-sized dried beans or peas such
as lentils, limas, kidney beans; barley or elbow
macaroni.

Short (two-foot) and long (five-foot) pieces of
rope, yarn or string. These can be attached to
toys for hand-over-hand pulling of toys up onto
a high chair or sofa.

Large, empty thread spools for stacking, stringing,
rolling and inserting into containers.

Plain clothespins.

cloth for book pages

elastic in assorted widths

old, clean toothbrushes; hair brushes

*sponges; cotton plush or "fake fur";
pieces of assorted fabrics*

*old buckle belts which can be cut
up*

*large snaps or fasteners set onto
small (1" x 2") rectangles of
material*

*small zippers from discarded skirts
or blouse tops*

plastic or metal curtain rings

jingle bells

*sewing needles and strong thread or
yarn; pinking shears for cutting
cloth pages*

*wire hangers; wire clippers for
home-made mobiles; adhesive tape
to cover scratchy wire edges where
necessary*

egg boxes

*nontoxic paints; crayons; paste;
Magic Markers*

*old, clean nylon stockings or foam
rubber for stuffing toys; beans for
stuffing bean bags*

Use a large coffee can, gaily painted on the outside. One or two clothespins are painted or drawn on the outside of the can. Clothespins are pegged all around the top rim of the can. Baby can practice releasing objects from grasp, filling up the can, pouring objects out of the can all at once and taking them out one by one. Paint all clothespins that belong to one can the same color as the clothespins painted on the outside of the can. If the infant becomes skilled at using a wide-mouthed jar, prepare a milk carton with a narrow mouth so that the game may be made harder. Contact paper rather than paint may be used for the outside of the containers.

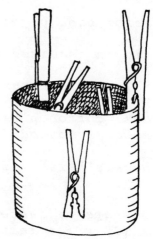

Use molded rubber sheets 1" thick from which puzzle-boards and pieces are cut. One, two, three or four-piece puzzles can be made. If desired, standard

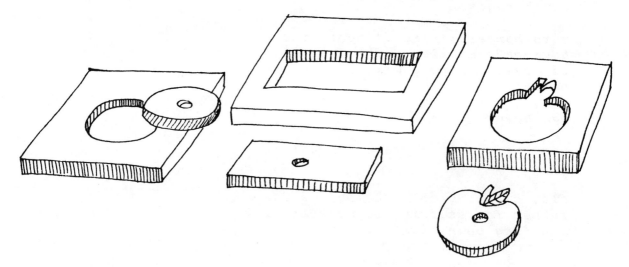

shapes such as circle, square, triangle, rectangle, may be cut from the rubber. Also, colored magazine pictures of single objects such as banana, apple or ball may be pasted firmly on rubber to conform to the contours of such items. Protect each picture puzzle piece with a coat of clear plastic nontoxic spray. Such puzzles may also be cut from thick cardboard or wood. More difficult two-piece puzzles may be made by cutting a large colored picture (of a dog or a boy or the like), mounted

2-piece boy puzzle

2-piece animal puzzle

on wood or cardboard, into top and bottom halves. We may cut a picture (of a dog, a horse, a couch, a jacket) into left and right halves that can be pushed together.

Orange juice cans of graduated sizes may be gaily painted and used as nesting or stacking toys. One set of three cans can be painted with blue polka dots on the outside of each can. Another set may be painted with vertical red and white stripes. This will make shelf replacement of toys easier, and also give cues to several toddlers who may be nesting or stacking cans so that they can recognize "their" cans on a table as they work.

Bottle caps, buttons and dried beans of assorted sizes should be sorted into separate screw-top jars and labeled. These would then be readily available for infants to practice grasping and releasing. _Such materials should be used when a caregiver is consistently present as babies try to mouth the items_.

A cloth book of items which facilitate fine-motor skills should be created by each trainee. Possible items at different levels of interest and difficulty for a cloth book are:

    A small zipper that can be pulled up and down
    is sewn on a page. Another zipper is sewn so
    that a horizontal pull and push is needed to

open and close the zipper. Large zipper pulls
are used for easier grasping.

A plastic 1" or 2" curtain ring with a 2" x 5"
terrycloth towel is sewn to a page. A baby
can hang up the towel by pulling the towel
through the loop. The towel is sewn to the
page at one end only.

A jeans-pocket is sewn onto a page. An infant
may turn the pocket inside-out and put something
into the pocket and then retrieve it.

A large snap and fastener, a single large button
and buttonhole, and a hook-and-eye on separate
cloth tapes are sewn each set to a page. Practice
in using fasteners and in easy buttoning is thus
made possible.

An oilcloth
shoe with
three lacing
holes and
laces
already
securely
double-threaded
into the bottom
hole is stitched
onto a page.

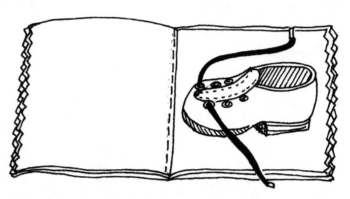

Two bands of
wide elastic
are sewn at
the midpoint
of each onto
facing pages.
Baby can grasp
either or both
ends and pull
one band
horizontally
and the other
vertically.

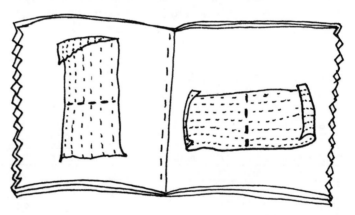

A rubber or plastic wheel from a discarded wheeled
toy is sewn to a page at its center so an infant
can push on the wheel to make it turn around.

A piece of plastic or rope clothesline is sewn at
each end of a page. A clothesline is threaded

with rubber
washers.
A baby can
move the
washers
individually
from left
to right
and back
again along
the
clothesline.

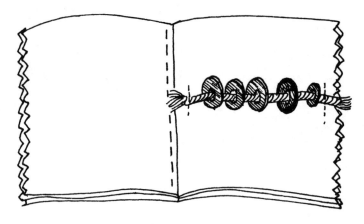

A dime-store ring is threaded on a piece of strong
elastic thread long enough so that baby can pull
the ring toward him and slip it on his finger and
off again.

5
SENSE EXPERIENCES

Real infants would be very helpful to the session on sense experiences. Trainees themselves, however, can be exposed to a wide variety of sensory experiences and learn from their own responses that an expanded world of sensation can be provided by a caregiver for sharpening an infant's knowledge of, and delight in, the colors, sights, tastes, feelings, sounds and smells of our world. Try to procure the following kinds of items:

- Wall mirrors and unbreakable hand mirrors.

- A portable hair dryer with both mildly warm and cool air settings.

- An old-fashioned washboard with wavy ridges.

- Soap bubble solution; rings and pipes to make bubbles.

- Finger paint (for nontoxic recipes, see Segner, p. 42).

- A tub of sawdust or sand -- the type that comes with a lid or hinged cover is preferable.

- Sifters, both the wide flat kind that you shake to sift, and the flour-sifter kind with a handle that turns to sift.

- Plastic bowl with tiny holes punched in the bottom through which water can drip slowly.

- Fragrant plants and flowers in pots or boxes for window sills.

- Large doll and tub of warm water with sponges and bar of soap.

- Swing set with suspended seat for an infant.

- Rocking (hobby) horse; rocking chairs for infants and adults.

- Assorted brushes -- soft and hard bristled. Toothbrushes, hair brushes, crumbing brushes and whisk brooms are suggested.

- Lamp with three-way bulb to provide different levels of bright light.

- A cage of soft furry animals (such as gerbils or hamsters) that would be easy for the day care staff to maintain.

- Small nylon, orlon or cotton stretch gloves or mittens.

- Balloons to blow up, tie at one end and sail across the room.

- Materials to make a book of "feelables," or a set of "touchables" and "clutchables." Plush, terrycloth, silk, chicken wire (with any sharp edges protected by tape), yarns, leather scraps, fur pieces (a rabbit skin sells for $1.00 in some shops), metal link chains (both belt and necklace widths), and sponges. Many clothing mail-order houses include free swatches of such materials along with their catalogs. Such swatches are fine for this collection.

- Soft receiving blankets for swaddling or cuddling babies. Soft cuddly toy animals.

- Music boxes; bells of different sizes and sounds; record player with records of sounds or children's songs; ticking clocks; rattles; chimes.

- A strobe light that can throw pulses of colored light on a child or on a wall in a darkened room, or light bulbs with flickering filaments.

- Similar items of different weights: A dense rubber ball and a lightweight ball; a heavier metal cup and spoon and a light plastic cup and spoon; two beanbags, one packed lightly and the other densely with pebbles or beans; a linked metal necklace and a linked plastic necklace.

➤ Foods with distinctive odors: Cut grapefruit,
   vanilla extract, ground cinnamon, fresh bread,
   for example.

The uses of some of these items are discussed in the chapters
on uses of living spaces and on Piagetian concepts. It is very
good for trainees to hear several times about all the ways a
caregiver can use materials.*

Ways In Which Babies Experience The World

Before you and the trainees begin to sample sensory experiences,
discuss with trainees the fact that even quite new babies are
sensitive to a variety of body sensations and experiences from
the outside world. Get the trainees to talk about various
sense experiences and how babies learn about their bodies and
the world around them from these sense experiences. Babies
respond to a wide variety of touches, sights, smells, tastes,
temperatures, body motions and positions, tickles and tones.
When they are very tiny, they may respond with much the same
overall bodily kicks or stretches or arm waves at first, to many
different kinds of stimulation. Only later does a baby learn
to act in particular and special ways to different kinds of
sensory stimuli that come from inside his body, or from the

*A few examples of books for babies which are commercially
available and which provide sensory-manipulative materials
or experiences within the book itself are: *Pat the Bunny*,
Golden Press; *All By Himself*, Plakie Toys; *Little Bunny
Follows His Nose*, Golden Press; *Touch Me Book*, Golden Press.
Further suggestions for books, records and materials for
infant sensory enhancement can be found in Parker, Huntington
and Provence (pp. 213-221).

outside world. When a tiny baby is hungry, he may thrash about
or cry. When a toddler is hungry, he may call urgently for *meat*,
or *cookie*, or *juice*, or *supper now*.

Sense Experiences For Trainees

The sensory stimulation should be designed so that <u>trainees</u> can
feel and experience awareness of and pleasure from their own
sense systems.* This will help them to understand the important
role of a caregiver in providing input and stimulation in order
that babies also may experience such sensory pleasures and
learn about the sounds and sights, colors and cuddles, sweets
and sours of life.

Stage each new sense experience so that one special sense is

stimulated. After a
while combine
sensation experiences.
Pour warm water or
sand through fingers;
hear songs or sounds;
smell vinegar or
cinnamon; have warm air
blown on wrists; be

*The chapter on Piagetian concepts of infant development
also provides examples of games and tasks a caregiver can
use to promote infant sensorimotor development. You may
wish to use some of those examples for further sensitizing
the trainees to the sensory enrichment potentialities of
Day Care experiences.

rubbed on the arm with rabbit fur or a toothbrush; have someone take your hand and move your open palm and fingers around the edges of a block, on a velvet cloth or down the ridges of a washboard while your eyes are closed. For each sensory stimulation situation you stage with the trainees or model for them, ask them to describe what they feel and experience, and which sense system is most actively involved in each episode. Later, as you turn to each new set of sensory materials (including the materials suggested earlier), ask the trainees to tell you which sense system will be primarily involved before you set about exploring the stimulating potentialities of the materials.

Feeding Several Senses Together

Combine some sense experiences, such as hearing and seeing, or looking and touching. Help the trainees discover that most of the time we get input into more than one sense system at a time. Adults enjoy the sight of a sizzling steak as well as the smell and the taste!

To provide the trainees with touching-and-seeing experiences, have them make fingerpaint patterns on glossy paper or paint with a solution of Ivory Soap Flakes and vegetable colors on a large oilcloth. Turn on a record, Chopin waltzes, for example, so that the trainees become aware of how the auditory input changes the mood and motions of their creations. For infants, these experiences may be even more intense than for

the trainees. Infants dressed only in diapers and exposed to
fingerpaints and a washable surface or a large glossy paper

tacked to a nursery floor may use elbows, behinds and arms as
well as fingers to produce a group "abstract" masterpiece! Or,
they can paint on their own.

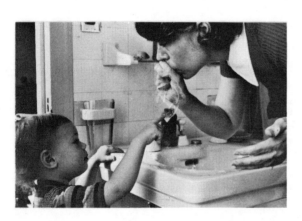

Blowing bubbles is another
multi-sensory activity. The
wet feel of a bubble bursting
on the palm, and the sight of
rainbow colors as a bubble
drifts glistening in the air
provide special looking and

feeling delights for infants -- and a bubble is simple to
provide. Can your trainees think of other ways they could use
the bubble-blowing activity in infant enrichment?

Sense And Motor Combinations

Trainees may now see ways in which rich sensory stimuli can be
presented and used to strengthen <u>motor</u> skills. If a toddler is

92

encouraged to "catch" the bubbles that a caregiver sends through the room, he will be able to coordinate looking and walking in such a way that he and a bubble arrive at the same place at the same time. He may have to stretch an arm or open a hand to reach for a bubble a bit too far from where he stands.

 Mobiles hung from walls and ceiling provide sources of sensory stimulation which can impel an inactive infant to stretch and reach (while held securely in his caregiver's arms) for the brightly-colored mobile hangings which swing in the air so freely at just a touch. A windup toy which consists of a gaily-dressed monkey who dances around in a circle and claps two small cymbals together may be fascinating enough so that a baby who can rarely be coaxed to practice creeping may, on his own, try to inch his way closer to the alluring toy.

Taking Advantage Of Daily Routines To Provide Sensory Input

Ask the trainees to tell you all the different kinds of sense experiences the following daily care situations can provide:

Meal time

Diapering

Bathing

Settling-to-sleep time

Dressing with outer clothing (or undressing)

Soothing a fretful infant

Make sure the trainees mention opportunities these routines
provide for infants to listen to the caregiver's voice; to
see, feel body pats or position shifts; smell, hear food
noises; and feel temperature and pressure changes on skin.
If the trainees have difficulty in imagining these situations,
you may provide them with large rubber dolls, bath powder,
tubs of warm water and diaper changer, so that they can act out
these caregiving routines. Ask them to vary their tempo and
style of handling a doll.

While bathing a baby one can rub his back vigorously with a
washcloth; one can squeeze water gently from the cloth onto
the baby's limbs as he watches; one can stroke the limbs
slowly and lightly in washing; one can splash lots of water
quickly all over his stomach and arms. Similarly, while
soothing a cranky baby, one can walk up and down the room

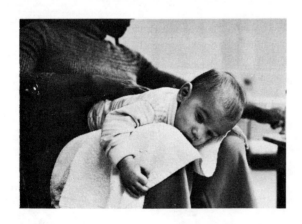

jiggling and jouncing an
infant; one can lay him on
his stomach and stroke his
back in large circular arm
movements; one can cuddle
him and rock him while
seated in a rocking chair;
one can whirl him around in arms quickly, hoping that the sudden
input of body (kinesthetic) stimulation will surprise him and
distract him from crying. A caregiver in her daily routines
also provides variety in food colors and textures. She gives

an infant experiences with feelings of different weights and pressures in many ways. An everyday situation can be used to explore with the child, for example, the weight of shoes and outer clothing being put on and off. Different caregivers will show different styles and timing in their handling of babies. Some babies respond better to certain kinds of handling. Trainees ought to be aware that while their style may be just fine for one baby, they may have to move a little slower or a little more vigorously in caring for another baby.

Let Baby Explore

Ask the trainees to think up daily care situations which provide sensory stimulation and experience. They will probably suggest putting babies on a rug surrounded by a variety of toys interesting to look at, to feel or to taste. Do they note that the caregiver can assist the very young infant by such a simple routine, for example, as a frequent change during the day in the infant's position? A baby needs some time

ALLOW THE BABY TO PROVIDE SENSORY EXPERIENCES FOR HIMSELF.

on a shoulder or a lap or some time propped in seated position in his crib or in an infant seat. If a tiny baby has some time on his stomach, either in a crib, a playpen or on a floor pad, he gets to see different samples of his visible world, and to practice exploring these wider horizons with his eyes. He also gets a chance to practice lifting his head, and later,

lifting his chest while supporting himself with his arms.
Provide a cradle gym with hand pulls hanging over the crib
where a baby's hand can grasp them. Let the trainees explain

how the cradle gym gives an infant
the opportunity to feel his own
muscles straining as he grasps and
pulls down on the cradle gym toys.
He can also stroke different textures
or scratch at smooth- and rough-
surfaced toys which have been attached
to a cradle gym with strings or
elastic bands.

Sensory Stimulation: Dosage

You have made clear what kinds of daily and special opportunities
the caregiver can provide for infant sensory experiences. Now
stage for the trainees a condition where too much sensory
stimulation is coming in for an adult's or an infant's comfort.
Have available a TV set or a portable radio or phonograph with
very loud rock music. Ask all the trainees but one to crowd
near each other and to talk loudly with each other and across
each other's heads. Also, turn on the TV or radio or
phonograph loudly for a couple of minutes. Then, turn off the
"noise" you have produced and ask each trainee just to talk to
her neighbor in a normal voice. Wait a few moments. Now ask
the trainee who was the silent one what she feels and what she

had felt in the midst of so many sounds and sights of different people. The trainee who has been overstimulated with noise and the press of people may describe more realistically to the group a frequent condition in overcrowded homes.

She may express the feeling of withdrawing on the inside from all that confusion. She may describe her feeling of relief when voices and crowding diminished so that she could hear individual people, or understand the messages of incoming voices.

Infants may be bombarded by too much noise and too many people rushing around or having loud discussions. Later on, when he is older, the baby who has lived in an overcrowded, confusing and noisy environment may learn to behave in noisy and overactive ways to produce his own stimulation where the surroundings have provided little orderly input to him personally. He may act so that his boisterous activities do count and are noticeable in the midst of the household confusion, even if the attention he attracts is negative. Have the trainees spend some time talking about how the Day Care Center must not overdose an infant with stimulation. Can the trainees think of situations where too many kinds and parts of toys would surround a

Explain to the trainees how important they will be as caregivers for monitoring the times and conditions under which babies get to know the world through all their senses.

97

baby so that he might not explore the properties of any one toy thoroughly? Can they see how a caregiver talking at or stimulating a baby too long a time may also be overstimulating him?

Sensations And Body Feelings

Explore with the trainees opportunities which occur in an infant's daily life where a caregiver can give emotional support to the infant in his experiencing of bodily sensations. If a caregiver caresses an infant, or rubs her cheek against his, or handles his bare skin with patient, tender hands, the infant learns from her muscle responses and facial expressions that his body and its sensations feel good to her, too. If the caregiver does not make unpleasant faces or remarks about thumbsucking or the smell of urine and feces, the baby will learn that his bodily functions are not disagreeable to the adult, as they are not disagreeable to himself. A caregiver may see a 2 year old on a diaper changer finger his genitals. If she casually accepts this activity, then the baby learns that what he feels as pleasurable is not associated with adult disapproval or punishment. Caregivers will find it much easier to socialize such an infant -- that is, to teach him adult ways, or more socially acceptable

CAREGIVERS WHO ACCEPT CALMLY A BABY'S PLEASURE AT HIS OWN BODY SENSATIONS WILL HELP A BABY TO GROW UP FEELING THAT HIS OWN BODY AND HIS BODY FEELINGS ARE ALL RIGHT.

98

ways of handling body functions or needs. The caregiver who accepts that her toddler enjoys walking about naked may find it easier to convince him that a supermarket aisle is not the place for such activity, but his bedroom or the breezy sunshine and privacy of a backyard is a good place, if she has a calm acceptance of the baby's pleasure in this and does not over-react to it.

Babies who have plenty of interesting sensory-motor experiences planned and provided for them by caregivers do not exhibit excessive self-stimulation such as thumb-sucking or masturbation for long periods of time. Tired or shy babies may need more of such self-produced pleasurable sensations to comfort themselves or to get used to strange places or people.

Summing Up Ideas About Sensory Experiences For Babies

Throughout this session, the trainees should learn to describe the kinds of sensory stimulation provided an infant by his caregivers and by himself. They may want to know some of the words for such experiences. Music provides an auditory input. Music can be heard. Being swung in a swing provides kinesthetic stimulation. An infant's body feels the swinging motion.

The trainees should have discussed and carried out a variety of activities and caregiving routines whereby one insures to an infant special, clear experiences in the rich world of the

Babies will show a startle reaction if suddenly dropped a few inches, or if a sharp sound such as a blaring horn or a hand clap occurs close to them.

They seem to quiet more easily if they are swaddled or snuggled in a soft receiving blanket.

They often seem to derive special pleasures from being rubbed gently all over with a towel after a bath, or from rubbing their cheeks and mouth area with soft fuzzy or furry items such as blankets, soft animals or pajama sleeves.

A crying baby will sometimes quiet rather suddenly or stop fretting if a music box, tinkling bell or other pleasant tones are sounded close to him.

They will croon or bounce their buttocks to rhythmic music.

Older babies will brighten at the sight of the bottle or a new toy, and especially at the sight of a loved caregiver's face.

Some older babies who have been introduced to baths and waterplay gradually and happily, seem to enjoy very long periods of play with water. A 2 year old can be the most enthusiastic volunteer for washing up utensils in soapy warm water that a caregiver could ever have.

Babies who are moving from strained to table foods will often express a preference for sitting with a caregiver and sampling the fascinating world of new tastes available on the adult's plate rather than his own foods, which have become too bland in texture and taste.

They sometimes show as much delight in squeezing and feeling foods of different textures as they do in tasting and swallowing the foods.

Babies like to sniff their world. They may lean close to a caregiver's arm to smell or even lick her skin. They may want to put their noses close to the pet turtle. They may be dazzled by colors and smells of flowers and plants in the Day Care Center or outdoors, or by the smell of fresh *baked goods from the Center kitchen.*

Their eyes become more alert if their body position is changed and they are brought up to a shoulder and held there.

Out on the playground or in a gymnasium, babies may like to be whirled around if firmly held, or have the caregiver push their swing seats into motion over and over again.

Babies like to feel and scratch and rub different textures and materials with their fingers. A baby may use his own body to provide such stimulation. He may suck on or stroke his sleeves or strands of hair.

Vary the amount and quality of sense experiences. A baby needs a certain amount of sensory stimulation to nourish his increasing interest in and exploration of his world. Too little experience is monotonous for him. Too much may make the world seem like a noisy, confusing place. Babies may "tune out" this confusion or they may become hyperactive and noisy themselves.

Be alert to individual differences. Babies differ in their needs for and tolerance of sensory stimulation. Some are comfortable with a cluttered living space. Other babies seem irritable when too many faces and voices and crowded furnishings surround them, or too many hands are handling them. Some babies can tolerate very talkative caregivers who busy themselves with a baby constantly. Others need plenty of free time -- time free of adult handling or talking -- when they can explore their world on their own. Cruising peacefully about a living room under and around furniture and even sampling a carpet crumb can provide a rich experience for a baby left on his own for a while.

Plan and schedule some sense experiences. If a baby is presented with too much or too new sensory stimulation, he may not be able to learn something clear about any part of the stimulation experiences. A sensory experience when planned offers opportunities for a baby to get information. For example, a music box may be offered to a baby for his viewing, then for his listening, then for his handling (or even tasting). Baby then has more of a chance to get information about various aspects of this new experience from each of his senses in turn. Or, we may offer a new experience for looking, hearing and touching at the same time -- a bright blue bracelet of jingle bells, for example -- but we offer one such item and not a heap

A CAREGIVER MUST BE ALERT TO HOW MUCH, WHEN AND WHAT KINDS OF SENSORY STIMULATION A BABY CAN BEST LEARN FROM AND ENJOY AT HIS GIVEN STAGE OF DEVELOPMENT AND AT A GIVEN TIME IN HIS DAILY LIVING PATTERNS.

103

of them at first. Body stroking and a lullaby are more
suitable at nap time than a record of jungle animal
calls. For a toddler, being outdoors on the grass with
his caregiver and with toys, slides and swings available
is preferable to spending the after-nap hours in a jump-
seat or empty crib.

Use caregiving routines to provide sense experiences.
Diapering, feeding and other caregiving activities
during the day offer many opportunities for enriching
the baby with sights and sounds and touches a caregiver
provides. Babies learn to know caregivers not only as
loving, helping people, but as special people who
provide interesting experiences for feeling, doing and
enjoying.

Accept baby's body functions and explorations.
Sensations provided by the baby's own body and body
functions are a natural part of his sensory experience
as he grows. The caregiver needs to accept calmly a
baby's pleasure at his own mouth sensations, or his
pleasure at touching his genitals. She needs to
respect his desire to enjoy sensations at times of his
own choosing. She must be careful not to overwhelm a
toddler with her wishes as to where and when his
toileting should occur. The infant's desire to please
a loved caregiver who appreciates his needs is a
powerful help to the caregiver who is weaning or
toilet-training a baby.

Coordinate sense and motor experiences. Sensory
experiences can be coordinated with newly-emerging
motor skills. Such combinations can enhance a baby's
interest in trying out skills in order to provide
himself with attractive sensory inputs such as tastes
and touches.

6

INFANT LANGUAGE LESSONS

The infant language training lessons can take place in a large group meeting, although from time to time trainees will form small groups to practice with a baby or doll. The trainees should invite mothers who are friends and neighbors to come in after the first few language meetings. Try to invite babies who are less than a half-year, one year, one-and-a-half years old, and 2-3 years old. Each mother will be asked to demonstrate her special ways of getting her baby to coo, babble or talk. The trainees will be able to practice language games discussed in earlier language sessions. The focus of the earlier sessions will be on language development and language learning with infants. The later sessions will involve reading to babies, selection of appropriate materials, and creation of some picture books by trainees.

Advance Preparations For Language Lessons

Purchase musical-sound toys. (A grocery carton makes a good storage box.)

Gather an assortment of safe, home-found materials for baby to make noises: Plastic bowls, empty metal coffee cans and tablespoons **are suggested items.**

Arrange for guest babies of assorted ages.

If no practice babies at all can be invited to your training session, you will need to prepare video-tapes of adult talking games with babies or to prepare to show a segment of film containing such conversational games. Caldwell's film, *How Babies Learn*, contains excellent sequences of adults providing language models for infants and eliciting vocalizations from babies in loving interactions. Another good film is *Abby's First Two Years*. This film shows baby's interactions with her mother and other children, her skill learning and especially her language development month by month.*

Have a tape recorder available. A cartridge model might be easy for the trainees to learn to use.

Provide a record player and an assortment of records containing chants, lullabies, poems and songs for young children.*

Section 1, Language Learning Sessions

Begin the first morning session by asking the trainees to talk about ways in which a baby communicates with a caregiver, how he makes known his wants, his likes or dislikes. If the trainees fail to mention a variety of communicating gestures and sounds, you may suggest a few, such as:

➡ Squeals of joy when you kiss his bare stomach and rub your face on it.

➡ Frowns and turning away of the head if his face is washed too roughly.

➡ Crying when hungry or wet, or when needing to be burped.

➡ Making sounds if he sees or hears something interesting and attractive.

➡ Raising his arms and grunting to be picked up.

➡ Pointing to the cracker box on a shelf and whimpering or tugging at the caregiver's clothes

*These films are available on rental from the New York University Film Library.

*Suggestions for selecting and using such materials: Schaefer and Aronson, sections entitled "Essay on Books;" Parker, Huntington and Provence, pp. 213-218; Painter, pp. 69-81.

to get her to give him a cracker.

How Vocalizing Begins

Talk about the development of baby talking. In the early months, for the most part, babies coo. They make throaty vowel sounds. Demonstrate a few, such as *uh* or *ahh*. Consonant sounds gradually come in, mixing with these vowel sounds. Sound a few consonants -- *d, g, m*. *Dlth* is a funny sound some 4 month olds make by vocalizing while the tongue is stuck out through a mostly-closed mouth. *Ngg, ba* and, of course, the well-known *ma* and *da* also come in over the next few months. When the baby is saying a long string of vowels and consonants mixed together, we call this *babbling*. Ask the trainees to give you some other examples of consonant-vowel combinations babies might make in the second half of the first year. If they have any difficulties, then play a tape recording of babies saying *da-da-da* and *guh-guh* and *bah-bah-bah*. The

BABIES NEED TO BE SHOWN THAT THEIR "TALKING" IN THIS FIRST YEAR IS IMPORTANT TO THE GROWNUPS WHO TAKE CARE OF THEM.

caregiver can show that the baby's early sounds and talking are special to her by repeating them back to the baby, or by smiling and talking back to the baby when he makes sounds, that is, when he vocalizes.

If no live models are available, play your already-prepared

108

video-tape of such "conversations" between adults and babies to show how the caregiver, by talking to baby as she pats his tummy and pays attention to him, encourages the baby to vocalize. Show the sequence in Caldwell's film, *How Babies Learn*, of such back and forth talking between a baby and his nurse-caregiver. This film episode will make clear to the trainees how such conversations can be started and kept up.

Caregiver imitation of baby's sounds will provide pleasure for the older baby who has already begun on his own to experiment with consonant-vowel combinations, such as *da-da* or *ma-ma*. Imitating baby's sounds also gives him the opportunity to produce his sounds when he hears them from others as well as himself. Getting baby to produce special sounds and special words, when you ask him for them, gives him a boost in his early language learning.

Words As Tools To Make Things Happen

Older infants who do not use words for food or for toys or for their clothing can get frustrated and cranky when adults don't understand their gestures or grunts. If a baby learns to use words he can feel good about his ability to get what he wants in his world. He can feel pleased about himself that people understand him. He is a

FEELING HE CAN MAKE A DIFFERENCE IN WHAT HAPPENS TO HIM ("MOMMY, COAT OFF," "MORE COOKIE!" FOR EXAMPLE) HELPS BABY'S SELF-CONFIDENCE.

person who can say things that matter. If he can ask for *milk* or *wa-wa* (water), or *juice* when he is thirsty, the baby feels he can act on the outside world and get his needs taken care of. As a result, the baby who has been helped to learn words for things he wants, for actions he is doing, for feelings he is showing, learns more easily to trust adults. He is also learning that adults -- parents and teachers -- are people one can ask for help or explanations. The baby who knows the names for some toys, animals or clothes in his world can be more sociable and friendly with his caregiving adult. He can show her his "doggie" with real pleasure. The adult, also changed by this early communication, responds appropriately to the baby more often and can help him promptly when he uses words.

Language Games For Trainees

Ask your trainees for single words babies might find very useful to know to get help or attention from adults. Make sure the following categories are included which will bring about caregiver assistance, comfort, praise or explanations:

Toileting words.

Clothing and clothing-fastener words (e.g., "shoe," "snap").

Food words.

Accident words (e.g., "sore," "bump").

Words to get adults to name things or to read (e.g., "What's that?," "book").

Socialization words (e.g., "up," "mine," "please," "kiss," "all gone").

110

Tell your trainees these are words to use a lot with babies while taking care of them. Make slips of paper with games like the following written on them:

Lift a baby into arms and say, "up we go."

Lift a baby down from a diaper-changing table and say, "Down we go."

Put arms lovingly around baby and say, "Mm, Janey gets a big <u>hug</u>."

When a toddler clutches at his pants, ask him, "Potty, Tommy? Do you need to go potty?"

If a baby chews food, say, "Nyum, nyum, nyum; Joey <u>eats</u> his food;" and make mouth motions of eating.

Hand baby a snack while saying the food word distinctly, "Cracker, Janey."

If a toddler is reaching for, or picking up a toy, say the name of the toy: "Judy, want the doll?" "Darren got the <u>car</u>."

Give the trainees the slips of paper you have prepared. Ask them to act out the situations. They may use a doll or each other to play the part of baby, depending on the situation. Ask them to think of and act out other similar caregiving situations where words can be taught.

Give out slips of paper with situations where the language used would overwhelm a baby: "Shabella, your pants are so wet. Why didn't you tell me that you had to go to the toilet? I would have taken you." "That's a pretty animal in the book. He's called a dog. He has four legs, a tail, and a lot of fur." Ask what other, simpler ways words could have been used to help the baby learn names for actions or pictures.

Ask your trainees what kind of voice they prefer listening to. Give examples of one that drones on and on, and one that goes loud and soft, one that tells you about things some of the time and also one that questions you some of the time. Most of the trainees will prefer the more interesting voice. Babies too love variety in the voices of caregivers. Babies love someone who whispers occasionally, or makes funny noises, or talks in a deep or a sing-song voice some of the time. Voice changes and different tones increase baby's awareness of the pleasure in the world of sounds. Babies sometimes startle or cry if talked to in a harsh voice. The soft sounds of lullabies have been used to soothe babies by all peoples for ages. Funny sounds, such as buzzing like a bee, hissing like a snake or burbling *glub glub* sounds as if you were under water can be used to attract a baby to watch your mouth as you make sounds -- and they amuse him as well. Demonstrate some funny noises and sounds with each other or with a guest baby. Animal noises such as *meh meh* or *woof woof* or *meow* intrigue babies. If one of the visiting mothers is already present, have the mother hold baby comfortably on her lap facing away from her. Ask trainees to come up one at a time and practice voice variety for the baby (for about a half minute). Let each try a whisper, an artificially deep voice, a change to a high-pitched voice, a questioning voice or other sounds with the baby. Ask the trainees to talk about what they observe. Does the baby look back intently at the speaker? If the baby turns away, which sounds seem to bring his eyes back to the speaker? Now, ask the speaker to switch to a placid, non-moving, non-talking face, and stare at the baby. Let the trainees describe for you how the unvarying face and voice seem to turn off baby's attention.

Songs

Teach the trainees some simple songs and lullabies for infants and toddlers. You may use records. Print the words on sheets and mimeograph a personal copy for each trainee. Read the words aloud for each song or chant or lullaby. Keep the tunes simple. Have some short (2 lines) and some longer songs. Some of the songs should involve teacher and infant in motion games. *Ring Around A Rosy* or *Itsy, Bitsy Spider* are examples of motion games played while a song is sung. Demonstrate

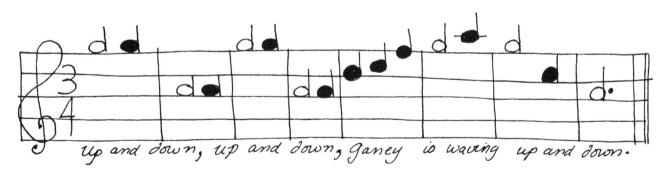

Up and down, up and down, Janey is waving up and down.

a simple motion song which uses the child's own name, such as: *Up and down, up and down, Janey is waving up and down.*

The demonstration should include all the important motions

naturally with the rhythm of the song. Be sure the baby is
facing you, either on lap or floor. Hold the baby's

hands and lift his hands up and put them down at baby's sides
three times in the course of the song. Each motion corresponds
to the appropriate word in the song. Ask the trainees to
practice with a large doll or a real baby. Show them how to
hesitate just a bit before singing the word *up*, and to smile
at the baby to give him a chance to say *up* before the adult
does.

Tape Recorder Use

Ask the trainees to sing or chant songs they know which babies
and toddlers might enjoy. Tape record the songs and identify
each one with the trainee's name. These songs can be part of
a music library for the babies. Appreciate each trainee's
offering. Ask for suggestions as to how use of the tape
recorder can alert a baby to his own new words. They may
suggest tape recording a toddler singing his own crooning song,
or a group game song such as *Where Is Thumbkin?* Children who
verbalize infrequently can be rewarded for talking by hearing

their own vocalizings and sayings played back to them on the tape recorder. This experience will be pleasing to them.

Making Sounds And Music

Ask the trainees to suggest other ways besides singing and voice tones which can provide a variety of sounds for a baby to hear. Make sure you get to talk about playing music boxes, turning on radio music, playing phonograph records, ringing chimes or bells, playing a xylophone, jingling a tambourine, and beating simple rhythms on a drum. Set out some of these materials and ask the trainees to practice making different sounds and rhythms with them. Ask each trainee in turn to call out some materials found in the home which babies might commonly see and which could be used to produce tones, sounds and rhythms which are interesting. If necessary, keep the game going yourself by suggesting the use of plastic, paper, wooden and metal items:

■➜ Rattling newspapers; crumpling cellophane.

■➜ Banging on an empty coffee tin with a metal spoon; clicking two wooden spoons together.

■➜ Pouring water into glasses. Also clinking with a metal spoon on glasses or bottles filled to different heights with water.

■➜ Shaking or rattling a plastic cup in a pot.

■➜ Hitting two empty toilet paper or paper towel rolls together.

■➜ Dropping an empty spool of thread into an empty plastic or metal bowl.

Have the trainees demonstrate sound and rhythm-making with a box of such assorted home-found toys. Ask them to verbalize

words like "clinkety clink clink" while dropping assorted
items into a pie tin or a pot.

Role-Playing With Babies

The trainees are now ready to work with some of the guest babies
invited to the training session with their mothers. Ask some
of the trainees to explain to the mothers what kinds of games
will be played with the babies. Accept the trainees'
explanations and sum up their points about responding to baby's
sounds and words; creating a varied and interesting environment
of sounds, vocalizations, words and music for babies; and
urging babies with smiles and talk to respond to sounds, to
words and to songs. Invite a mother and a 5-7-month-old baby
to show the trainees how to get "conversation" going between a
caregiver and a young baby. This should be a good demonstration
of language stimulation. Ask the trainees to describe how the
mother is getting her baby to vocalize. Make sure they have
noted that mother leans forward and looks right at the baby, and
that the baby is looking right back at her. Mother may nod her
head and smile or caress the baby as well as say sounds back to
him when he vocalizes to her. Ask the trainees about the
mother's voice pitch. Does it move upward or downward as she
says nice things to her baby? Ask the mother if some of the
group can try talking back and forth with the baby. Trainees
may then practice stimulating the baby to enjoy (pay attention
to and smile at) adult vocalizations and make sounds himself.
Make sure the baby isn't over-stimulated by too many adults.

116

Keep the trainees who are not working with the baby to the side or in back of the infant so they do not distract him. Try to keep laughs and side conversation to a minimum.

While the volunteer baby is seated on his mother's lap, ask a trainee to approach from the back on the right or left side alternately and quietly to stimulate the baby with an interesting sound. She may turn on a music box, or jingle a bracelet of small bells, or play a triangle. Ask the trainees to watch what happens. The baby should turn toward a new sound, and often will look alert and attentive. He may bounce his body to rhythmic sounds. He may reach with his hands to obtain the jingle bells or music box.

Arrange for a mother and an 8 to 14-month old baby to talk to each other. Have the mother sit comfortably in a rocking chair and hold her baby so they look at each other. Ask her to "talk" to her baby -- for example, to tell him he's a big boy, or to tell him how handsome he looks all dressed up to meet the people there. Or, if the mother has some special tricks she uses to start her baby talking with her, have her use them. Ask the mother to imitate her baby's vocalizations whatever they are. Let the trainees tell you what they hear. Does the mother repeat exactly what the baby says? Does she try to sharpen the sounds that may be closer to *dyuh-dyuh*, for example, so that she repeats *da-da* clearly, and gets the baby to imitate her back again with a sound more like *da-da*. Does the mother move very far from the

baby's level of vocalization? That is, if the baby is saying
da-da, ask the mother to try to get him now to say *ba-ba*, or
syllables close to the ones he can say. What happens? Ask
the trainees to watch the baby's eyes and mouth. See if he
tries to move his lips and face to accomodate to the new
sound, that is, to make his mouth parts close and open to make
the new sound rather than the old one. If the baby does try
hard with his mouth and tongue to make a new sound such as
ba-ba, ask the mother to try a word or sound which is not at
all like the ones he can make (*bread* or *balloons*, for example).
Let the trainees tell you what the baby does. He may look
at the mother's mouth and face, but then quickly lose interest
and turn away, or even start a new game by poking his finger
in her mouth! Explain that this new sound was too <u>different</u>
from the sounds he has learned, or is working at learning, to
make. When we want to teach a baby new sounds or words, it is
best to stay close to sound combinations with which he is
familiar. We move only slightly away from the known sounds
or words in teaching new ones to a young baby.

Early in the second year the baby may start imitating many
different new words and sounds, even when he doesn't understand
what they mean. Repeating words after his caregiver will be a
fun game for him. Then it will be easier for the trainees to
teach new sounds and words by pointing to things and giving them
names, that is, *labeling* objects, or toys, or foods, or body
parts, or pictures for the baby.

Action Words

Ask a couple of trainees to sit on the floor on a rug with a 12-month-old infant. The trainees will *say special words while the baby himself is doing something or acting* in a special way. For example, if one of the babies visiting the training session bangs on the floor or on a feeding table in which he is seated, have one of the trainees nod and smile, and say *boom, boom, boom* or *bang, bang, bang* as the baby bangs his hand or a toy on the surface. If the baby looks up surprised and then repeats the banging, ask the trainee to *label* the baby's action again. Let her do this a few times, and then repeat the action herself -- that is, bang on the table while calling her own actions, *bang, bang, bang*, and getting the baby to watch. The baby will begin to connect the word she is using with the action of banging. After a few sessions, sometimes over days, sometimes at the end of a 10-minute session, the baby can be asked to *make bang, bang, bang* while he is <u>not</u> banging. The trainee should watch for signs that the <u>word</u> may start the baby banging. If the baby still does not begin to connect the sound to his arm movements, suggest to the trainee that she hold his hands, smile, and chant *bang, bang, bang* for him as she gently and rhythmically does the arm motion to go with the words. The baby will enjoy the game. *He will have more chances to hear a word that stands for something he is doing.*

This game may also be played in order to show a baby how to

make sounds and how to listen to them. Trainees label sounds

for babies while they and babies make the sounds, and then ask

the baby to produce the sound by
its name. As a baby plays a
xylophone with a stick, the
trainer chants, *"La, la, la,*
Davey's making la, la, la."
When the baby stops playing,
she may reactivate him by
urging, *"Make la, la, la, Davey;*

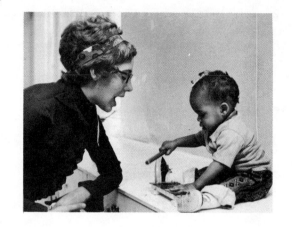

play la, la, la," as she demonstrates xylophone playing once

more. Ask the trainees to think of other simple games a baby

can play where the caregiver can attach a label or a name to

the game. When the trainees offer their ideas for these

games-with-words, ask them to tell or show <u>how</u> they would

begin to teach the baby. Make sure they understand that new

words come slowly. The baby will first learn to do the action

or a part of the action that the word suggests. He may pronounce

the new sound or word poorly. Only later will he be able to use

the word for himself to tell the caregiver what he is doing, or

what he wants. Make sure the trainees tell you that they would

follow up their baby's gestural and vocal efforts with a smile,

a hug or words of appreciation and praise for the baby. Don't

let them expect rapid learning. Experience at this level is

important. Don't let them get caught in success and failure

judgements.

Break trainees up into small groups of two to practice games with each other. If you have arranged for enough babies from 6 **to 18** months to be present, let the trainees break into groups of three each to one baby. One trainee at a time may try a word game with a baby.

The object of the games is to attach sounds or names to actions, and then to ask the baby to do that action by using the sound name you have given to the action. With the slightly older baby, games of "kick the ball," or "roll the ball," may be tried. The caregiver says the words every time she shows the baby how to do it. She says the words every time the baby tries to do the action.

With babies in the second year of life, a wider variety of action words can be taught. To teach the word *around* to a toddler, you could:

STRESS THE IMPORTANCE OF USING DIFFERENT KINDS OF ACTIONS TO TEACH ALL NEW WORDS.

➤ Swivel the seated baby around and around slowly and gently on the floor, while chanting *around and around*.

➤ With a walking baby, play *Ring Around A Rosy* while singing.

➤ Roll your head around in a slow circular motion. Ask the baby to roll his head *around and around*. Say the words as you repeat the action.

➤ Help the toddler mix some instant pudding in a bowl. Take his arm and stir the pudding. Chant *around and around* as you guide his stirring. Pause so he can "fill in" with the chanted word.

➤ Give him an egg beater to turn *around and around*.

➤ Give him a Magic Marker or large crayon. Demonstrate

drawing circles *around and around*. Use the words and
encourage him to draw *around and around*.

■——→ Spin a wheel on an upturned trike around. Then ask the
toddler to make the wheel go *around and around*.

Go around the table asking each trainee to show with her hands,
words and any props she needs, how she would teach the following action-word phrases:

put in	take off	see doggie
put on	take out	see baby
show me	sit down	say bye-bye
pick up	close	splish-splash
go get	push	wash
give me	dance	eat
pat	pull	hug or kiss
write	point to	pat-a-cake
		try to

If a trainee suggests just teaching the action-word with one
kind of toy or in one kind of situation, praise her suggestion.
Then ask for other kinds of games or situations which would
help the baby learn both to say the action word, and to carry
out a caregiver's request to do that special action. Ask a
trainee what she would do if the baby didn't try to carry out
the gesture. How can she help the baby try? [For example,
if a noncreeping baby were asked to *get the wind-up toy*, but
it was placed more than a foot away from him, he might not
comply. If it were placed too close to his hand, he might grab

it before the caregiver could ask him to *go get the toy*. If it
is placed just far enough so the baby has to stretch a bit for
it, or swivel his body to get it, then his reaching action will
be associated with the words *go get*. His action can be praised.
Sometimes if a trainee puts her hands gently over the baby's
hands, she can demonstrate an action such as *pull* or *push* more
easily.]

Quality Words

Older babies can learn qualities of objects and people as well
as action words. Adjectives are quality words that describe
objects and people. Give the trainees a few quality words, such
as *short, dry, wiggly*. Adverbs are quality words that describe
when or where or how or why actions are carried out.

Hand out a mimeographed sheet of adjectives and ask the trainees
which they would try to teach toddlers. Spread out an
assortment of objects which a trainee might use with a baby to
help teach some quality words: A small metal-ridged washboard
for "bumpy," a pot of water for "wet," some Scotch tape for
"sticky." Let the trainees think up as many ways as they can
to teach these quality words and others they suggest themselves.

Teach the trainees the "So Big" game to play with their arms.
Show them how to use their own bodies to exaggerate gestures
and facial expressions to convey the meaning of a word like

"heavy" or "soft," so that a baby can better understand the quality word being taught.

When And Where And How Words (Adverbs)

Very slowly, over the first two or three years, infants develop a sense of how their living space is organized or when events occur. Toddlers in a Day Care Center may be well adapted to a very familiar routine of outdoor play, then lunch and then nap time. They know words for sleep or nap or eating. Yet if they are asked, "What will we do now <u>after</u> we finish our play on the swings, or <u>after</u> we eat lunch," they often cannot put their daily routines in the proper sequence. They will guess a wild variety of activities. Thus, trainees must not expect that babies will easily understand phrases such as, "Your turn is next, or later," "<u>Soon</u> we will clean up for snack," "Color on the <u>outside</u> of the paper plate," "Walk <u>slowly</u>," "Turn the handle and <u>then</u> push the door." Get the trainees to talk about physical actions which would help the baby understand some time or space concepts -- such as slow, fast, under, over, here. Words that describe how actions are carried out will be easier to teach. Ask the trainees to explain why this is so. Be sure they give you some examples of contrasting-action situations which a caregiver can set up to teach quality words, whether adjectives <u>or</u> adverbs.

Baby bangs on the table top hard with a hammer; the adult models *hard*, and calls the action *banging hard*. Then she taps softly

and calls it *banging softly* or *gently*. She may hold the baby's
hand and help him feel the difference in effort involved in
banging one way compared to the other. A sponge filled with
water may help the baby learn this concept too. If he squeezes
hard, a lot of water comes out. If he squeezes gently, very
little water comes out. Try a contrasting talking situation
with *loud* and *soft*. Have a trainer ask a 2-3 year old to talk
in a loud voice. Let her raise her voice to show him what
loud means. Then have her talk in a soft voice and ask the
toddler to speak softly.

Name Games

Many toddlers are ready to learn new names -- for people, for
body parts, for toys, for furniture or animals. Ask the
trainees to call the babies and each other by name frequently.
A baby should get familiar with his name so he looks up when
his name is used. Ask the trainees whether they consider it
as easy for a baby to learn words like "dog," or "door" or
"dolly," while seeing or touching these in the real world, or
as toys, or as pictures in a book. Praise the trainees for
their good guesses. Learning names for actual creatures and
things is easiest. Learning to name pictures is harder.
Dramatize for the trainees a funny episode in which you may
have a 15-month-old baby in a feeding table. You are trying
hard to get him to point to and say "shoe" to the correct

picture in a set of clothing pictures. Suddenly, you are kicked lightly. The baby has lifted his foot outward from under the tabletop to show you "shoe." He has <u>tried</u> to comply with your urgings, but is not yet used to showing or labeling (naming) pictures.

If the baby did not yet know how to show his shoe, or teacher's shoe on being asked, would we expect him to be able to point to a picture of a shoe? The trainees' answer to this question should lead naturally to a discussion of <u>how</u> we can judge when babies are ready to learn words for food, furnishings, toys, pictures or concepts such as *top* or *corner*.

Now you are ready to stage a naming game. A couple of trainees are to sit on the floor. First, one will play the role of the baby as realistically as possible, and the other will play the caregiver. Then they can switch roles. The first game can be learning body-part names. A large doll should be available. The caregiver points out "baby's" body parts and doll's body parts and her own body parts. She asks the "baby," "Now show

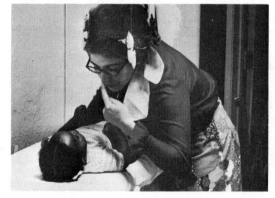

me dolly's hair. Pretty hair." She can also urge the baby to

"Comb dolly's hair." If the "baby" is playing her role well, she may instead feel the caregiver's hair! The trainees will enjoy the "mistake." Does the caregiver correct "baby" gently, point again and explain, "That's Miss Day's hair. This is dolly's hair?"

If the caregiver asks the "baby" to show her own ears, a "baby" who is in the swing of this game may instead point to her own eyes. The caregiver should (with a straight face, if possible) hold the "baby's" hands on ears and label, "Ears. These are your ears." Then the caregiver moves "baby's" hands correctly and gently says, "Eyes. Here are your eyes."

Once the trainees have gotten the flavor of this game, let them triple up with a doll. One trainee should be an alert observer, while two others role-play the teaching of body-part names. Each of the trainees should get a chance to play each role. Circulate among the groups. One "baby" may decide to act very advanced and quickly carry out all appropriate gestural responses, as well as label correctly. Does her caregiver then ask you for additional materials, such as a different, smaller doll, or pictorial materials with which to continue this game?

This game can also be played in order to teach clothing, foods, room parts or household items. Demonstrate with a real baby how you could play a variant of the name game, such as the following:

In front of the baby, seated on floor or in feeding table, spread out a group of food items and utensils, such as spoon, plastic cup, empty milk quart carton, plastic glass. As the baby reaches for or snatches up an item, point to it, or touch it and name it for him. After you have named the items a few times, take from a paper bag of identical items next to you an item that matches the one he is handling at the moment. Hold up your cup, for example. Point to his cup, and then to your cup and say, "Cup," each time. Exchange cups with the baby and point with a smile to cups you have traded. Say, "See, Johnny's cup, Betty's cup." Pretend to eat from the spoon, or to drink from your cup or milk carton and name what you are doing and the item you are handling.

Section II, Reading Skills For Infants

How babies can grow up happily interested in words and pictures in books is the focus of these sessions. Whenever possible, real toddlers, 11 months to 3 years of age should be invited for practice book reading. The trainer will need an assortment of books suitable for babies, and stacks of different kinds of old magazines. Construction paper, cloth, glue or tape, string or yarn, scissors, and cardboards will all be needed for book-making activities. Most of this session will be activity-oriented.

The very title of this training session may puzzle your trainees.

Find out what they think this might mean. To hear, to say, to see words should all be positive experiences for the growing baby. If a caregiver is usually silent or uses words harshly or negatively much of the time, babies do not have good experiences with words. When people

FIND WAYS TO MAKE BOOKS WITH PICTURES AND WORDS A SPECIAL AND PLEASURABLE EXPERIENCE FROM INFANCY ONWARD.

who are important to baby, people he loves, show an interest in reading, whether books or boxtops, babies learn to value written words and pictures. Reading behaviors are easily imitated. Caregivers play the same role that parents play in reading. When a parent sits down with an evening paper or a weekly magazine, a toddler is likely to go search out a book of his own and sit himself down next to the parent to "read" -- even if he holds his book upside-down initially! What is important is that the baby chooses and shows himself a book just like the grownup does.

How To Promote Reading Readiness

Make certain that the trainees see that there is a connection between learning to read easily and more quickly in elementary school, and the earliest experiences of enjoyment with pictures, words and books. The caregiver who sits down and reads a book with baby gives him a chance to see interesting pictures and hear a story or words that go with the pictures. Books or magazines, labels, recipes on food cans, storefront advertisements and street corner signs are a unique way of learning in life.

Just as the toddler learns from caregivers, from his own activities, from toys and from playmates, so can he enrich his experience of the world with books and written words.

Making Infant Books

Show the trainees an assortment of commercial books, such as *Baby See*, cloth alphabet books, and some homemade books you have prepared. Heap a variety of magazines, cloths, cardboards, paste, scissors and ribbons on the floor. Ask the trainees to flip through the magazine pages and tell you which magazines seem to have pictures most suitable for making baby books. Praise them for their efforts to find large, simple colorful pictures which relate to baby's life experiences and interests. Check to see that the trainees choose pictures that represent male as well as female persons. Pictures where a man is hammering a nail, or smiling at a woman and child, or driving a car, are as important as pictures of mothers, children, toys, animals or food. The trainees should choose pictures of persons of different ethnic backgrounds and persons of different ages. Pictures of a baby, a grandmother, a father and a whole family at a picnic can be used for a four-page book. Ask the trainees which kinds of books they will need: A single-subject (different foods, clothing items, room parts, etc.) book, or varied. They will probably decide both kinds are good to have.

Uncluttered single-item pictures with bright colors are easiest for babies to recognize. Group pictures or ones with small figures are confusing to the very young baby. If any trainee is having difficulty choosing pictures, bring her attention to some of the magazines where she has a better chance of finding appropriate pictures. When each trainee has made one or two cloth or cardboard books, you will be ready for the final work of the afternoon.

Role-Playing Reading Skills

The trainees, using their own and commercial books, now can practice in groups of three, some of the teaching skills with books they have learned. First, demonstrate picture-describing rather than story-reading for the very young baby. Then demonstrate story-reading for the older toddler, where hand or body motions are involved. Show how to get the toddler to *wiggle* like the fish in the story, or *blow* on the dandelion puff like the children in another story. The trainees will take turns at playing "baby," caregiver who is reading or observer who can make  suggestions. A "baby" who is playing her role well will require the caregiver to practice her skills at holding pages open when fumbling hands try to fold the pages. By good acting, a trainee "baby" can also get the adult reading to her to make funny noises or voice changes to recapture baby's wandering attention. If real babies are available, two trainees and one baby and mother may form a group to practice reading skills.

Let the trainees talk freely about their experiences making books and showing and reading picture-books to babies. Stress how pleased you are with their first book productions. Say how glad they should be to think that with their help a baby by one year can learn to *go for* books with bright pictures and words, just as he *goes for* an enticing toy, a dish of applesauce or a whirl-around hug from his caregiver.

A-boom.   The caregiver sits facing baby on the floor.
If he cannot sit well, the baby may be in an infant
seat in front of her.   The caregiver leans forward
and touches foreheads with the baby.   She says, "A-
boom."   As she does so, she smiles or laughs for the
baby.   The object of the game is to get the baby to
lean his forehead forward ready to bump foreheads
gently with the caregiver when he hears her say, "Want
to play A-boom?"   A good way to start this game is to
watch for a moment when the baby leans forward by
himself.   Then meet him by leaning forward yourself
and calling out, "A-boom!"

Shake, shake, shake.   Many babies midway in the first
year can shake or wave a large piece of paper **or a**
cloth or a rattle handed to them.   When the baby does
this action, or gesture, the caregiver calls out,
"Jimmy, shake, shake, shake."   She smiles and may
shake her arm up and down just the way the baby does,
imitating his gesture.   If she labels his action often
enough, he will come to learn that what he does with
the piece of paper is called shake.   When he has
begun to be familiar with this word, the caregiver can
offer the baby a large piece of paper and urge him,
before he does anything with it, to "Shake, shake,
shake the paper."   If he then does the action right
after her words, the caregiver should praise the
baby.   "Good for Jimmy.   Jimmy can shake, shake,
shake the paper."   She can then give the baby a
rattle and ask him to "shake, shake, shake."   Changing
the toy this way helps the baby to learn that shake
means what he is doing with his arm.   The word
doesn't just belong to paper or rattles.

Up.   When the baby raises his arms to be picked up in
the latter half of the first year, ask the caregiver
to say, "Up.   Mary wants to go up," to the baby just
before the baby is picked up.   When the caregiver
holds a baby way up from her body so that he can touch
a mobile, or reach for a wall decoration, ask the
caregiver to say, "Up we go," as she swings the baby
upward from herself.

Peek-a-boo.   The caregiver may try any way she likes
to play this game.   She may call out "peek-a-boo" as

she drops a diaper over the baby's head as he lies on his back so that the diaper hides his eyes. When he removes the cloth, she may clap and smile for baby, saying, "I see Jamey." Or she may sit facing the baby, who is in a feeding table, and then lower her head slowly below the tabletop level, saying, "Peek-a-boo," and then pop up into the baby's view again, saying, "I see you." She may hide partially behind a tall piece of furniture, such as a dresser, or behind the edge of a door, and say, "Jamey, I'm hiding." Then she can pop her head back so the crawling or seated baby can see her face again, and say, "Here I am...peek-a-boo!" If the baby wants to, let him throw a diaper over the caregiver's head or face. Say as he does so, "Jamie plays peek-a-boo," and then exclaim, "There we are," or some words of surprise and joy in the game as either he or she pushes or pulls the covering off her face. As the baby gets used to playing peek-a-boo when the caregiver asks him to, he may put his hands near his eyes and laugh, or drape a diaper on his head without fully covering his eyes. He may creep behind a couch so that he is partially hidden. The caregiver calls out, "Where is Jimmy hiding?" After he comes from behind the furniture and grins, say, "Peek-a-boo, I see you!" Accept his variations on the game. The caregiver may want to ask an older baby, who plays readily when he hears the words, to play peek-a-boo with <u>another</u> person, or with a teddy bear, or with a doll. Hand the baby a diaper and say, "Play peek-a-boo, teddy bear." The baby will enjoy the novelty of playing the game by hiding the toy animal with the diaper. If he does not start the game, show him how. Hide the toy animal and say the game words. The baby will also be learning that the word stands for a game of hiding and sudden reappearance, and not just for one special action he does.

Ding-a-ling, ding, ding, ding. For a year-old baby, the caregiver can clang a metal spoon back and forth in a metal pot to make a ringing sound. As the baby sits and watches, the caregiver sings, "Ding-a-ling, ding, ding, ding," (in musical thirds) as she clangs the spoon back and forth. She tilts the pot so that the baby can watch the motion that produces the ringing sound. Then she places the spoon in front of the baby with the handle facing him, and holds the pot tilting toward him. She urges the baby, "Danny, make ding-a-ling, ding, ding, ding." If the baby does not try, or simply bangs with the spoon on the *pot, the caregiver shows him again how to clang the spoon. She again sings the words as she does this, and then again offers the spoon to the baby and urges him to go "Ding-a-ling, ding, ding, ding," with the spoon.*

Quality Words

Which words would <u>not</u> be appropriate to teach toddlers and why? Which would be easy because the caregiver can think of actions to go along with the quality words she is teaching?

soft	wet	selfish	tired
brave	bad	big	hot
sticky	gentle	dirty	good
wooden	cold	slow	happy
more	fuzzy	pretty	big
smooth	shiny	purple	heavy

Talk to baby as you play with him, as you take care of him, as you tidy a room or do other work.

Work from where you find the baby in his language learning. If he is good at "ga ga," move to "ba ba" or "bottle," but not to "bundle" or "barometer." If he has lots of single words, try to build in 2-word phrases ("Milk all gone." "Pretty shoes."), but do not work for long sentences right away.

Take advantage of when the baby shows interest or attention or exploration behaviors with new items in order to teach new words.

Accompany new words you are using with an appropriate action.

Use a variety of actions to teach new words.

Use words clearly and briefly when pointing to new items or actions or places.

Give a variety of smiles, hand claps, praises and hugs, as well as return conversation for baby's spontaneous vocalizations, his imitations of new words, his labeling actions or items for you. Show your enjoyment of baby's "talking" whether it consists of his lengthy babbling or rough approximations of names like "baw" for "ball," or "wainee!" for "It's raining!"

Find out whether baby has learned the meaning of a word well by seeing in how many different situations he can understand the new word correctly. For example, can he: Pick up a book, point out a book among other objects, carry books, open a book, etc.?

Have a special place for picture books, homemade or bought, for infants. A baby who has "his" special books at home can learn to feel proud of and protective of his treasures. Toddlers in the Day Care Center should know where they can go to find a book to show a grownup or to look at quietly on their own.

When you read initially to a baby, use a picture book. Label a few pictures of items already familiar to him in his everyday life. Dog, baby, ball, car, shoe, soda, apple, mommy, cookie, light, juice, bathtub, are some good pictures for early books. A three-page book with three large bright colorful pictures, one per page, may be sufficient for an 11 month old. By three years some toddlers can easily enjoy a twenty-page picture book with stories or poems.

Make reading a warm emotional experience. If guest babies are present, show how a trainee can rest two infants on a comfortable couch on either side of herself and hold the book on her lap. Demonstrate how to cuddle an infant on a lap in a rocking chair while reading with him. Use dolls for props if no infants are available.

Talk about the reading experience while it goes on with a baby. A trainee should say to the child, "Now we'll open our book." She should point to pictures and label them. Baby may mislabel a picture; for example, he may say "woof-woof" to a cat picture. Just have the trainee say, "See the kitty-cat. Meow! Kitty-cat." With an older baby she may say simply, "Yes, it looks like a dog but it is a cat." Also, she may explain the difference between a cat and a dog. Have her ask baby to point to the cat or show it to her. He may then label "cat" or "meow" correctly. She should praise him and smile, repeating his words after him. If he points to a body part he knows (the eye, for instance) of the animal, have her accept this with pleasure and say the word for the body part.

Make sure the trainee doesn't linger longer than baby seems comfortable with on any one page of the book. Have her ask a baby to help "turn the page." Show her how to hook an adult finger quietly under a page so a single page is turned by the baby. Ask her to

thank a baby for helping to "turn the page." Urge a
trainee who is practicing reading to a baby to
express surprise at one of the pictures in the book,
if that item is familiar to a baby, and ask, "What's
that?" If a baby names the picture correctly have
the trainee repeat the label with a confirming voice
and hug or praise the baby. Such a technique
increases baby's pleasure at his own competence.
When a trainee and baby are finished with the book,
have the trainee let the baby help her close the book.
She should tell him, "We read a book. Now we close
the book. Good for Joey. Joey read a book."

Tell trainees not to criticize poor articulation.
"Airpay" from a 2 year old should get an approving,
"Yes, an airplane. It flies way up in the sky. An
airplane, Joey," from the caregiver.

Make sure the trainees pronounce words clearly for a
baby. If the doll in a picture book has a hand and
hair and hat, the baby may only say "haya" for each.
The caregiver must pronounce the final word sounds
firmly, as she points out the doll parts in the
picture. Then if she asks baby to show her a hat,
she will be less likely to have the baby look
up questioningly as he asks "haya?"

138

Ask the trainees to remember to vary voice tone in
reading just as in conversing with baby. When they
show a picture of a puppy leaping up to catch a
ball, they should let their voices rise in pitch to
say, "See the puppy *jumping*. Puppy is *jumping* up to
get the ball." If a kitten is pictured sleeping in
a basket, they can use a low voice, or even break
into a whisper, to say, "There's the kitten *fast*
asleep. Such a tired kitten. She's sleeping in her
basket. See how quiet the mommy cat is. Kitty is
sleeping."

Have the trainees encourage a baby to point out
things to them in a book. The baby is learning that
adults who share his pleasure in the book are in a
special caring and teaching relationship with him.
The young toddler needs a caregiver to read books
with him and to tell him about the pictures. But he
also needs an adult to comment simply for him about
those pictures he himself finds amusing or odd, such
as exaggerated whiskers on a cat, old-fashioned boots,
etc. A baby's trust in an adult as helper with books
and words and pictures, as someone interested in what
he points out, is important in shaping his early
interest in reading materials.

Tell the trainees that while they are working in the
Day Care Center a toddler may bring a book to "read"
while the adult is on her way to diaper another baby.
Each trainee should try to find time with the child
to point out, and show interest in at least one
picture-with-words, even though she may be busy. If
necessary, she can promise, "Harry, I will read your
book with you as soon as I finish diapering Lynn."
The caregiver who then sits down to read with a
toddler (or two) a few minutes later has shown that
she finds the baby's request for book-time important.
Incidentally, this is an excellent "action" way to
teach the time concept "soon" to a toddler.

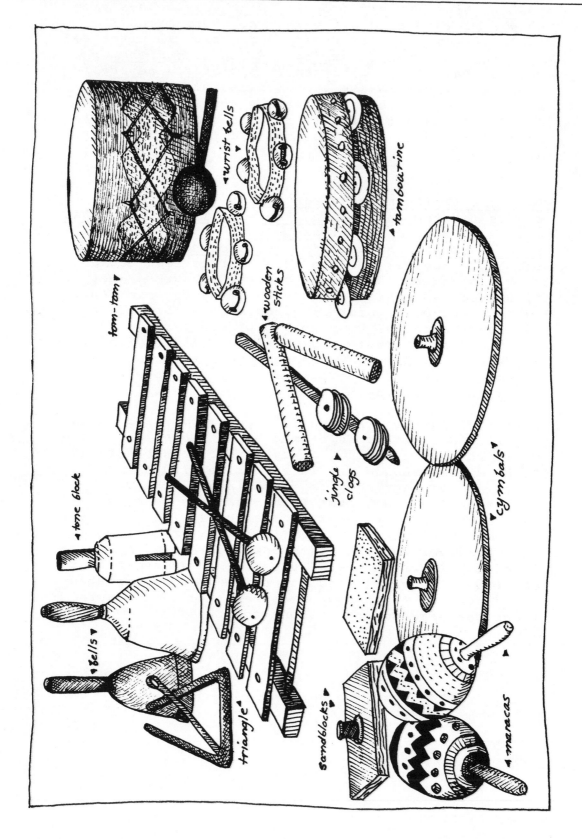

7
UNDERSTANDING PIAGET

This chapter in many ways stands apart from all the rest because it concerns itself with the work of only one man, Jean Piaget. People "understand" Piaget on many levels, and his theories of child development are difficult ones to comprehend completely. Because we feel that at least a familiarization with his theory is a necessary experience for every child care worker, and because he is the most prominent person in the field of child development today, we will use this chapter to present briefly Piaget's thoughts on child development.

To begin to understand the theories of Piaget you must first know something of Piaget, the man. Jean Piaget was born August 9, 1896, in Switzerland, where he still lives. As a young child he was interested in nature and enjoyed observing animals in their natural surroundings. He was a very bright young boy, and had his first article published in a natural history magazine at the age of eleven. As an adolescent scholar, he broadened his interests to include not only biology, but also philosophy, religion and logic. A special interest of his was epistemology -- the branch of philosophy concerned with the study of knowledge. Epistemologists study how we organize our thoughts and ideas when we try to describe the real world around us where objects and people exist in space and time. Piaget received a doctorate in science at age 21,

and then studied child psychology for four years. His interest
in logical thinking carried through to his work with children,
and he became fascinated by "wrong" answers children would give
on tests of intelligence. He began to see a pattern in the
thoughts of children and became aware of the fact that children
under 11 years of age could not carry out certain logical
operations performed easily by most adults. He believed human
thought developed along biological lines, and that the quality
of intellectual processes actually changed as one matured.
Early in his work, he adopted the theory that the thinking
of children differs from adults in two ways: Children and
adults differ in the amount they can understand, and more
importantly, the thinking structures of children are actually
different from those of adults so that it is impossible for
them to understand certain things as adults do. Although the
structures differ, the same kind of learning process is at work
from infancy onward, no matter what new knowledge is being
gained.

The formulation and evolution of human knowledge fascinated
him. He felt that if one hoped to understand adult thought,
one must study the child. Development was a process of formation
and evolution. A major question of his could have been, "How
does a human being adapt himself to his environment and learn
skills which will in turn help him to learn more about his
environment and then even more complex skills?"

Piaget, who is now over 75 years old, has been working during the last thirty years testing and experimenting with his theory. He remains active in the field, and his work today on memory is as exciting and as important as his early work. Still a major leader in the field, he is at present concluding another book on child growth and development.*

Unless you have at least a full week to devote to Piagetian theory, concepts and tasks, you should plan to use the pre-service training sessions to highlight the main Piagetian developmental advances of infants which occur in the first 3 years of life. Avoid using complicated Piagetian terms such as "pre-operational period" or "recognitory assimilation." Spend a good deal of time having guest babies model different infant responses to Piagetian tasks. Hand out sheets describing some of the Piagetian tasks (presented later in this chapter) in the different developmental areas. Model the presentation of these tasks yourself and ask the trainees to role-play these presentations. Later, during the in-service training sessions, use films* to define some of Piaget's terms, and talk more about special ideas of Piaget.

*See Ginsburg and Opper, pp. 1-85; and Baldwin, Chapter 6, "Piaget's Description of Development During Infancy."

*An excellent choice would be the series of six films, *Ordinal Scales of Infant Psychological Development*, distributed by Dr. J. McV. Hunt and Dr. I. C. Uzgiris. The films, which may be rented from Visual Aids Service, University of Illinois, Urbana, Illinois, depict many Piagetian problem situations. The sequences of Piagetian developmental advances in the sensorimotor period are
[continued on next page]

Section I, Piaget's Theory Of Child Development

We cannot, of course, do justice to Piaget in one chapter, but a general understanding of his overall theory will make easier work with the particular activities presented later. Piaget sees development broken into three large periods. A brief outline follows at the end of this chapter.

People are often confused when reading Piaget by the "strange terms" that he uses. Actually once you begin to become familiar with Piaget's definitions of these terms, your understanding of his theory will be broadened. We do not advise that trainers stress or even use these "strange terms" in their training. They <u>do</u> <u>not</u> have to be memorized by the trainees. We do, however, define some of these terms (following the chart of intellectual development) to help the trainer with her background reading.

Use the history presented above and the outline to introduce the trainees to Piaget. Spend some time discussing some of the Piagetian ideas and concepts. Several different possible

presented in detail. A film, *Guiding Environmental Discovery*, which demonstrates ways of encouraging infant curiosity based on Piagetian ideas is for rental from Dr. R. Formanek of Hofstra University. Her film, *Two Babies*, compares a full-term with a premature infant on a variety of Piagetian tasks. Three films, *Object Permanence, Spatial Relationships* and *Causality*, by Dr. S. Escalona, are available from the New York University Film Library. They depict aspects of sensorimotor development occurring between 4 and 22 months and the behaviors that characterize each Piagetian stage of development.

teaching and training techniques to get these ideas across are discussed in this chapter. One difficulty with teaching Piagetian theory is that people often react to the theory as they do to Latin and statistics. Purposely keep the discussion low-key and informal and do not try to impress the trainees with all the new terms you have learned. If you see a negative or resistant tone being set, quickly move to work with babies or dolls on the activities described below.

Give the trainees some good examples of baby actions and try to explore the "point," or the developmental idea, which your example is trying to illustrate. The next section includes some samples from different developmental areas* of this "example to idea" method of training, and is followed by other methods of training.

Section II, Training Methods
Training Method One: "Example To Idea"

Please refer to the outline and definitions in the material at the end of this chapter as often as you feel the need. Try to get the trainees involved on a concrete level in these activities. Use infants to illustrate the activities. The examples below each describe a different area of Piagetian development, but by no means include all of the possible behaviors in the different

*Assessment techniques, available from Dr. Sibylle Escalona, Drs. Hunt and Uzgiris, Dr. Lawrence Kohlberg and the Syracuse University Children's Center, describe various levels of Piagetian tasks in each of these developmental areas with instructions for administration.

areas. The examples are:

Infant Development Of The Concept Of Object Permanence [1.]

When a baby reaches Piagetian stage 4 of the sensori-motor period, Piaget describes how well the baby now can actively look for and find a toy that is entirely hidden under a cover such as a sweater or a piece of cloth. An object which disappears from his sight has begun to take on the quality of permanence. The baby is prompted to search actively around where the object disappeared, not only with his eyes as in stage 3, but with his hands also. However, at this stage, what happens if a caregiver, who has been slowly making a toy disappear several times under a sweater to the left of the baby and coaxing baby to get his toy, now moves the toy underneath another cover to the right of the baby? The baby watches the caregiver's hand movements, and watches the toy disappear under the new cover. Then he turns and looks for his toy in the place where it was before, namely, under the sweater.

After you describe the above example of behavior from Stage 4, ask the trainees to discuss the incident. Does the baby's behavior show any advance over his previous ability with hidden objects? The trainees will remember the baby's inability to find a totally hidden toy in the months before this. They will remember that up till now the baby needed either to have a partial glimpse of his toy sticking out from under the cover or still to be clutching his toy when a cover was thrown over it in order for him to get the toy out from under the cover. However, the trainees should

point out to you that the infant still seems unable to take into account the different movements of an object being hidden in a new place. He still acts as if the object's position has some special personal relation to his own previous action (looking under the sweater). The trainees should conclude with the idea that for the infant from 8 to 12 months, objects are still not completely objective realities outside the baby's own body and responses. He has not yet learned to recognize that objects are permanent and have an existence which is independent of his own actions.

Infant Development Of Actions That Go Together [2.]

When a baby is in Stage 1 (from 0 to about 1 month of age) of the sensorimotor period, if he hears a caregiver talking lovingly beside him or shaking a rattle near one ear, he moves his body so the adult is quite sure the baby has heard the sound. In Stage 2 (from about 1 to 4 months of age) the baby will make clumsy and then more skillful efforts to get his eyes and head where they can see the person or toy making a sound.

The trainees should express the clear idea that what the baby has gained in this episode is the knowledge that *some sights and sounds go together* -- such as a caregiver's face and open mouth plus loving talk. He learns to coordinate basic actions of looking, hearing and touching. A musical rattle can be seen and heard and handled and tasted.

INFORMATION ABOUT SOME PART OF THE BABY'S WORLD CAN COME FROM DIFFERENT ACTIONS.

Infant Development Of Grasping Skills [3.]

*When a baby takes his first swipes at mobiles hanging
over his crib or shakes bells dangling from his
wristband, his first arm and hand motions are very
clumsy. He seems to set the toys in motion more or
less accidentally. As he sees or hears what happens,
he seems to begin to connect his actions with those
interesting events that are happening. He keeps on
making arm motions, and seems to get better and better
at carrying out the arm motions or hand motions
required. He gurgles and smiles as he keeps the mobile
hangings in motion.*

The trainees should gather from this description of a baby in

Stage 3 (from about 4 to 8 months) that babies in this stage

begin to connect some of their accidentally carried out actions

with the interesting sounds and sights which accompany the

action. The baby now tries to repeat

what was interesting -- an important

concept for the trainees to understand.

Babies work hard to repeat interesting

*P*RACTICE IS A
PLEASURE FOR AN
INFANT.

results of their actions. Through trial and error they develop

more effective and precise actions. Their arm and hand movements

become more regular and more skillful with practice. That is,

the baby seems to adapt the force and direction of his motions

as well as the parts of his fingers and wrist and hand he uses

to the situation so that he can keep the interesting show going

on.

*Infant Development In Understanding Causal Relationships
[4.]*

*The caregiver winds up a mechanical toy animal by means
of its key. She gets the toy animal on the floor and*

she and baby watch the animal dance in circles. When the toy stops, baby picks up the toy without looking for the key to turn or trying any other procedure which might make the toy work. He gives the toy back to the caregiver and waits expectantly for her to make the animal dance again.

The trainees should bring out the idea that although this baby does not yet understand causal relationships, he can now anticipate an event that will happen. This is an important step in baby's learning to make sense out of his world. Ask the trainees to think about other signs a baby can now give that he is expecting events to happen. For example, about this time, babies learn to associate the sight of a well-liked bit of food on a spoon with the taste. Babies open their mouths in anticipation of some foods. Just as expertly now they close their mouths before a caregiver can bring a spoonful of nonpreferred food to their lips. Babies who start to cry if they see mother putting on a coat are also showing their new ability to interpret signals and anticipate what is going to happen. Mother-with-coat-on has come to mean mother will leave the house for a while. A baby's crying here is a good clue to his ability to interpret the significance of some actions and anticipate the events that will take place.

The trainees will remember that when the baby was under 4 months, if he saw a toy in motion he had no understanding of what caused it to move. Baby was just as likely to move his own limbs vigorously when the toy stopped. He then acted as if his own actions even at a distance from the toy were enough to "cause" the toy to move again. Baby has now begun to look for causes for actions outside his own body. Our clue to this step forward is his handing the toy to his caregiver to set in motion. Ask the trainees what step they would next expect the baby to take as he grows and understands more about the causes of how toys work. Express your pleasure if they suggest that later on baby may watch intently as a caregiver turns the wind-up key to make the toy animal perform. Then he may try to imitate her and work the key himself. Turning may be too hard for him at first. Later on, if a trainee takes a similar toy and winds it up behind her back before setting the toy down to amuse the baby, the baby who is in Stage 6 (18 to 24 months) will pick up the toy when it stops and then look actively for a special place to turn or push in order to get the toy working again. Learning that the world doesn't act by magic or by his own wishes is an important gain of the first two years of living. Helping a baby to look for what makes something happen or how something can be made to happen is an important part of a caregiver's job. Ask the trainees, "What kinds of toys would be useful to help a baby explore how things work?" Praise them for suggesting jack-in-the-boxes, music boxes, friction cars, toy telephones that ring when dialed, and other such toys where baby has to search for a way to pull, or turn or press a special part to make something interesting happen.

When babies are tiny, they haven't a good idea of how far or near things are to them. They may even lie in a crib and reach up to touch the shining moon! A baby later on may sit in a high chair with a pile of toys his caregiver has set in front of him. He drops one toy over the side of his chair and stares at where it falls. Then he leans forward and throws a toy in front of him. He follows that toy too, with his eyes. Next, he may throw a toy hard so it falls further away on the floor.

The trainees, in discussing this example, may remark that this kind of behavior, so often considered a nuisance by busy mothers, seems to be very purposeful. Baby seems to be trying out drops and throws to see where things go. He discovers where "near" and "far" are in space by his experimenting with different amounts of effort and different placing (sometimes not very accurate) of his toys as he lets them go. Ask the trainees for other examples of how babies discover what space is like.

*B*ABIES NEED TO "DISCOVER" FACTS ABOUT SPACE BY THEIR ACTIONS.

If they have trouble thinking of examples, ask them to remember what young babies do if a favorite ball rolls under a low piece of furniture. Only by Stage 5 or 6 (that is, toward the middle of his second year) will baby develop a pretty good idea that *space is continuous and there are different paths to get to the same place.* The baby, with more experience (and probably some bumps from trying to push through or under a solid piece of furniture), now looks at his ball and trots around the piece of furniture in order to reach the place to which the ball has rolled.

The trainees should comment to you at some point during these examples that development of sensorimotor concepts such as "what space is like" or "how causes and effects work" seem to be gradual. And in the sensorimotor period they are still making their discoveries in the world of actions. They cannot yet deal with these discoveries using only ideas or mental images. Explain that these new mental

ONLY SLOWLY AND WITH MANY EFFORTS DO BABIES DISCOVER HOW THEIR WORLD WORKS.

discoveries will take place in the period from 2 to 7 years, when young children become capable of imagining or thinking about what can happen without having to carry out the actual actions. To "imagine" means to have a mental picture of some specific action or event. A 3 year old can tell you if his ball falls off the table it will bounce on the floor and roll for a while. He doesn't need to do the action in order to imagine the series of events which will happen.

Infant Development With Regard To The Separation Of Means-Ends Relationships [6.]

A baby is seated in front of two square cotton crib pads, one on either side of him. Two-foot strings sewn to the front of each pad are stretched across the table so that one string lies conveniently near each of his hands. The caregiver attracts baby's attention with a shiny new toy car. Then she places the toy on top of the left pad and urges baby to go get the car. He tries hard to reach for it directly but the car is too far from his hand. The caregiver taps and jiggles the pad and string, and invites baby to use these to get the car. He finally tugs the string and moves the pad so he can get the car. When the caregiver tries the game with the right hand pad, the baby uses the string after a couple of tries at direct reaching.

The trainees should express clearly that this baby is now able to use some of his actions as means which are separated from goal actions such as picking up a toy to play with or mouth. The trainees may be alert to the fact that in other games this baby may still go for a toy directly without trying to use a

convenient or necessary means such as a support or string or tool. Also, they may ask what would happen if the caregiver now placed the toy between the two pads or held the toy slightly above one pad. Baby may still pull the support by its string without attention to the lack of contact which now exists between toy and support. Caregivers must be alert to the many different levels of learning. Some babies are just starting to separate actions as means or ends. Some cannot be fooled by a "trick" such as the one described above. They would try again to reach directly for the shiny toy or to ask the caregiver for it, once the toy is no longer obtainable by means of the support.

Infant Development Of Imitation [7.]

A caregiver seated facing her baby on a rug is playing pat-a-cake. The baby is laughing and imitating caregiver's hand claps quite nicely. Then the caregiver stops the clapping games and shows the baby slowly how she crooks or wiggles her fingers. Baby stares at his hands. He moves all his fingers a bit and looks doubtful. The caregiver keeps showing him the funny new gesture. Gently and with smiles she encourages him to try this funny finger wiggle. He tries and then grins as she nods and praises his efforts. Next the caregiver tries to wink her eye. Baby turns serious and stares at her face. As she continues to "perform" for him, he loses interest and creeps to her lap to be snuggled.

The trainees should all note that pat-a-cake involved a gesture which was familiar to baby and which he could see. The new gesture which involved wiggling fingers was not one baby had done exactly that way before. But it was close to other hand gestures he knew, such as waving bye-bye. Also, he could watch his hands. Thus it was easier for him to keep trying and to get a pretty close imitation of his caregiver.

GESTURES AND ACTIONS WHICH A BABY KNOWS ALREADY AND WHICH HE CAN SEE ARE THE EASIEST FOR HIM TO LEARN TO IMITATE DELIBERATELY.

The trainees may point out that the caregiver's next new gesture
-- winking -- was not one the baby could see. Nor was it one
he had done before himself. It is too hard to learn a new
action which is very different from the ones already practiced.

Ask the trainees, "If the caregiver had
wanted to teach an action invisible to
the baby, what kind of action would
have been easier to teach?" The
trainees may suggest mouth opening or
hair pulling. Babies by one year are
familiar with these two actions and

*IMITATING A FAMILIAR
UNSEEN ACTION IS
EASIER THAN
IMITATING AN
UNFAMILIAR UNSEEN
ACTION.*

have carried them out themselves even though these are actions
they may never have watched themselves make. Imitations aren't
perfect at the start. Babies work at getting their actions
gradually closer and closer to what the adult model is doing.
Not until Stage 5 (12 to 18 months) does baby show systematic
efforts in his tries at imitating whatever gestures an adult
models for him.

According to Piaget a baby who is at the end of the six stages
of the sensorimotor period (from birth to about 18-24 months)
is also ready to do something else special because he is
beginning to be capable of having mental images. The baby can
now imitate some action of an adult after the model is no
longer present. Sometimes, after a caregiver has been playing
a new imitation game with baby and later peeks in to see if
he is settling down in his crib at nap time, she may be amused

to discover him patting his cheek or performing some other new gestural game they had played together earlier in the day.

Mental Images: An Important New Advance For Baby [8.]

A baby is seated surrounded by toys and cuddly animals. He picks up a small spoon and makes scooping motions as if he is filling the spoon with something. Then he puts the teaspoon near his teddy bear's mouth. The baby smacks his lips and says, "Nyum, nyum," for his toy animal, as if it were making satisfied sounds while eating.

The mental image of which the older infant is now capable makes possible the first use of real "pretending" play. For example, this baby now can "pretend" his toy animals are eating. Baby behavior can now be used to represent something else. We call this "symbolic" behavior. Baby can pretend to read a book and murmur to himself while doing so. He can pretend to telephone mommy or Santa Claus with a toy telephone. Baby can now also pretend to carry out actions with new objects. He can use other kinds of toys or objects in his game and pretend they too are "telephones" into which he is talking. Of course, babies in the latter half of infancy don't always keep the boundaries clear between pretend games and real games. They may shift back and forth. But the new step for the baby is his ability to separate an action he really is doing from an action for which he has a mental image and he is pretending to do. This is an important step forward in the child's gradually learning how to use symbols in his thinking and in solving problems.

Training Method Two: The "Diagnosis"

Once you have gone through many examples of infant behavior in
each of the developmental areas which were illustrated above,
then get one pair of trainees at a time to role-play "caregiver"
and "baby" so that other trainees can "diagnose" the learning
situation.   If available, guest babies may be invited to play.
The trainees are then given turns to present Piagetian tasks
to babies of different ages and to vary the task level
depending on baby responses.   The other trainees stay behind
the baby and "diagnose" quietly how he is coping and what else
could be tried to help make the task easier or more complicated
depending on his responses.

Use the diagnosis method to have one trainee present a problem
to another acting as baby.   The object of the diagnosis now is
to describe developmentally what kind of response the baby is
role-playing.   For example, let one trainee present an "unseen-
hiding" problem.   A toy is hidden under a cover without the
baby's seeing the actual hiding.   A toy or bit of cracker may
be placed in a cup or in a closed fist, with the adult pouring
the object out quietly under a cover.   The baby watches the
cover lifting, but is not to see the object as it is poured
out or hidden.   Let the trainee who is role-playing "baby"
choose a response or action which either she or the other
trainees then have to explain and describe developmentally.

If the trainee "baby" looks only in the caregiver's hand or in the cup, what can the trainees tell each other and you about the "baby's" ability to deal with an unseen hiding problem? The trainees probably will want to see if the "baby" can handle a hiding problem with one or several covers when the toy is seen as it is covered. They may also want to see if, on further tries at the "unseen" hiding problem, the "baby" does make an attempt to search under the cover for the poured-out toy after searching the adult hand or cup. The trainees are probably tuned in by now to the possibility that a baby sometimes acts or fails to act on a level that a caregiver expects because of chance factors, such as lack of enough attention or an impulsive sudden interest in a detail not related to the problem. For example, the baby may start to look for the rest of the cracker from which the hidden bit was broken off. If the baby solves the unseen hiding problem with one cover, let the trainees decide what small change in the problem could be tried next. Would it be reasonable to expect that a baby who still looks in the adult hand before searching under the single cover can solve easily a problem where several covers are set out and a toy released by the unseen hiding method under one cover?

Another difficult diagnosis has often been called the "problem of the match." Adults who are sensitive to the problem of matching what they expect a baby to try with what a baby has already learned or done will be able to hold a baby's attention. If a new action required of a baby is too different from what

159

he has achieved developmentally he will find it too hard to
learn. The _adult_ must decide where her baby is able. She
should play games and set goals that require efforts which he
can make. If she sets tasks too difficult, a baby will "tune
out." If she repeats only the old
gestures or words, a baby will get

LEARNING SEEMS TO BE MOST "FUN" WHEN THE "NEW" IS NOT TOO DIFFERENT OR TOO DIFFICULT BUT OFFERS SOME CHALLENGE TO THE LEARNER.

bored. Thus, the wise caregiver
will learn from her babies. Each
one is an individual whose skills
and grasp of the world are at
somewhat different levels. In
trying to develop new skills with
her babies, the caregiver must take
these individual differences into account. Just as one baby
is not ready to creep when another is already toddling, so one
baby will not be ready for more varied and difficult imitation
games where his age-mate is already grinning and enjoying such
games.

How The Caregiver Learns To Make Good Matches

Let one trainee play baby. You model for the group some good
examples of how to adjust task levels to make an enjoyable and
good learning experience for an infant. For example, if you
are trying a game in the area of means-ends relationships, tie
a three-foot string to a toy. If your "baby" won't use the
string to pull in the toy, after several tries, detach the

string and offer the toy to the "baby." Let "baby" pretend to refuse this toy. Ask the trainees whether this horizontal short string problem was too hard for this "baby." The trainees will no doubt urge you to try a toy "baby" likes better. Try the game again. Let "baby" pull the toy in quickly now. Play this game over and over. See if the trainees will begin to object spontaneously, and tell you that the game in its present form is too easy. If they so comment, tie a long (eight-foot) string to the toy and stretch two other long strings out very close to the toy string on the table. Let "baby" act very impulsive and confused and pick up or pull incorrect strings. The trainees should be triumphantly calling out that you have forgotten to watch the match, and have made the string problem too hard too quickly for this "baby." Ask trainees to come up and try different ways to make the string problem a challenge, but not too hard all at once. Praise them for demonstrations which involve gradual lengthening of the attached string in different presentations of toys. Praise them for adding one confusing string at a time, and for lining up the toy string and the non-toy string clearly apart on the table at first. If the "baby" is not able to solve the problem of one horizontal long string because her tugs don't bring the toy close to her, ask the trainees what they would do. They may suggest showing the "baby" how to use a hand-over-hand pull to bring a long string in. They may use their own hands to help the "baby" do hand-over-hand pulling.

They may praise "baby's" clumsy initial efforts and encourage her
to keep trying.

Ways To End Learning Games Happily

Get the "baby" to act tired or cranky while the trainees are
trying to help her with the long string problem. Ask trainees
whether the learning game should be ended now. Trainees may
observe that it is better to end baby learning games in a
pleasant way. Ask for suggestions as to how to do this at
this time. A trainee may suggest going back to a shorter
string problem with a new toy, so that baby can experience his
own success and pleasure as well as caregiver praise at the
end of this string game. Express pleasure at various trainee
ideas which will end a learning game with a baby feeling good
about his own efforts and about the learning situation.

During the diagnosis sessions with real babies, trainees should
discuss whether the problem of the match is being adequately
met. Is the baby challenged sufficiently? Are the steps by
which the caregiver moves from easier to more difficult task
presentations small enough for this baby's learning comfort?
Does the baby show by his attention or vocalizations or
concentration that this is an enjoyable or interesting
experience for him? If a trainee is playing baby, give any
trainee a chance to take over the game who wants to try out
another way to re-interest "baby" or to vary the task. Trainees

who are comfortable with each other can also try switching roles in this way when real babies are present in order to modify a game or task to improve the match and increase babies' interest and efforts.

Training Method Three: The "Discovery"

Another good way for you to help trainees understand Piagetian ideas about infant development is to present them with learning situations for themselves where their own actions will illustrate Piagetian concepts about infant development. For example, buy a 30-cent wooden paddle with a small rubber ball attached to it by a rubber string for each trainee. Let each trainee practice using this paddle. The aim of the game is to hit the ball back up onto the paddle as many times without missing as you can. As the trainees practice, urge them to take note of their own actions and feelings. Ask some trainees to stop a while and watch others trying. After the session with the balls and paddles has been given sufficient practice time, talk with the trainees in order to get them to comment on what happened to them as they tried the ball and paddle game. The following major points about their experiences should be brought into the discussion in order to relate them to Piagetian ideas about infant development.

> There was an urge to keep on trying to do the new action. Active tries at learning were fundamental to improvement.

> If an accidental change in arm or hand posture seemed to make the ball go more accurately, then there was some

163

ability to use this feedback, to profit from this "accident," in order to produce the desired improvement.

Attempts were made to use familiar ways of moving the arm and using a hand grip as a means to the goal of skillful ball batting. There was intention to use familiar hand positions in the service of this new goal.

At times there was a deliberate attempt to vary the arm and hand actions in order to see what happened. New ways of holding the paddle or of moving the arm were tried out deliberately in order to discover solutions to the problem of increasing the number of perfect hits in a row. Making use of this ability to vary actions deliberately was a very important means by which increased control over the new skill could come about.

SUCH TRIAL AND ERROR EXPLORATIONS ARE AN IMPORTANT TOOL WHICH ENABLE A BABY TO COPE WITH MORE AND MORE DEMANDS OF HIS WORLD AS HE GROWS.

Sometimes a mental picture flashed in the mind and connected a previous action with its result. This remembering of what actions "worked" better helped shorten the learning process to improve the skill.

Despite the difficulties encountered, there was pleasure in learning and trying, in organizing information from mistakes or successes and in coordinating that information in order to better one's performance.

By these six observations trainees have expressed discoveries about their own efforts at learning which are very relevant to stages in the infant's learning career. Talk with trainees about the order in which some of these infant advances in development occur. For example, trying well-known and pleasurable actions out on new tasks or objects is common to

younger babies. By Stage 5 (12 to 18 months), babies
purposefully try out new ways to vary their actions and to
produce interesting results.

Training Method Four: "Make Up A Game"

Another method which you may use with the trainees, after they
have had lots of experiences watching you and each other carry
out Piagetian tasks with either role-playing trainees or with
real babies, is to ask each trainee to make up a game in a
given Piagetian developmental area. Each Piagetian game should
be spelled out in detail by a trainee. The aim of the game
should be stated. What the trainee would do if the game as
devised proved too hard or too easy for baby must be included.
After each trainee has contributed a game from one developmental
area, switch to another area and start collecting more games
from trainees. Below are two sample games made up to encourage
looking behaviors in infants under 6 months.

Alternate Glancing Game

The aim of the game is to help a baby under a half year of age
use his eyes to look at things actively in order to see them.
Present toys about 18 inches away from a baby's head as he
lies on his back. Present one toy several inches to the
right and one several inches to the left of his midline of
vision. At first you may need to call to the baby from the
left or right to get him to look at each toy. Or you may need

to move the toys closer together so he doesn't have to turn
his head or eyes much to see one toy and then the other, or
you may have to move one toy until it is in his line of sight,
or you may have to sew a jingle bell onto each dangling toy
to attract him by the sound as you shake the toy. Jingle
one toy. Wait for the baby to look at it. Jingle the other
toy. Wait for him to shift his glance. Wait to see if he
then looks from one to the other. If not, jingle each again
in turn to help him shift his gaze. If he can switch well,
try two other dangling objects, such as kitchen spatula,
striped soda straw, ring of keys, rattle, potholder, hand
mirror or other objects that sway or make a sound or reflect
light as they are moved to attract baby's attention.

Eye Tracking Game

The aim of this game is to help a baby follow moving objects
with his eyes. Another aim is to help him learn to look at
what he hears. Younger babies can lie on back or tummy. Older
babies may be seated. Twirl a shiny spoon or a bracelet of
little bells or a brightly-colored rattle until he focuses on
the object. Then move the object slowly in
one of the following paths: From left to
right, or right to left; from his chin down
towards his tummy or up towards the crown of
his head; in a 360° circle around the back
of his head in either direction ending up

again in front of him where he can see the toy well.

If the baby loses the toy with his eyes, help him "catch" the toy again by jiggling the toy or tapping it so it makes a sound. If he still finds following a bright-colored or jingling toy difficult, switch to the Human Object. Waggle your smiling face above his head. Then move your face downward toward his tummy. Make sure his eyes are on you. Bring your head back up toward his face. Move it above his face toward his crown, and then back to your starting place.

If the baby has trouble tracking your face, add sounds or chants, like *down, down, down we go*, as you move your head downward toward his feet; or make bubbling sounds with your lips as you circle his body with your head motions.

Tape record the trainees' games as they are described and explained. If possible during another session, bring in guest babies. Let trainees listen to a given game and try it out on a baby. If not enough details were given to do the game well, ask trainees to record further on tape what must be done. They may need to specify more precisely the goals of the game or tell how to vary the game with a baby who is either quick to perform or slow to catch on to the game's requirements.

At the end of this "make up a game" training procedure you may have the collection of games typed and handed back to the trainees in a booklet. This is their first homemade booklet of Piagetian games to play with babies. This "make up a game" exercise, where trainees comment on details possibly omitted by the trainee who is describing her game can be profitably used during in-service training. The method, along with creation of homemade materials, helps caregivers search actively and creatively themselves for new ways to activate babies to explore their environment and to discover new action patterns which they can use to enjoy and to find out more about their world.

Sensorimotor Period, 0-2 years

Stage 1
(0-1 month)
An infant uses the reflexes with which he enters the world. He sucks, sees, hears, cries and grasps.

Stage 2
(1-4 months)
The beginning of a life based on learning now appears. An infant begins to change his reflex behavior because of the experiences he has had in the new world in which he finds himself. He changes hearing to listening, passive seeing to active looking, and he begins to try to satisfy himself (by thumb-sucking) and to communicate (by different kinds of crying).

Stage 3
(4-8 months)
A baby begins to "feel" his effect on other things. He becomes interested in causing actions. His striking, rubbing, shaking and kicking seem to begin to have the purpose of making interesting or pleasurable events happen over and over again.

Stage 4
(8-12 months)
A baby will show unquestioned intention. He will pull a string in order to bring closer to himself an attractive toy attached to the string. He will use a stick as a tool to rake in objects out of his reach. Such "means" as the use of the stick or string are now used freely in the service of many different goals. A baby now begins to understand when his mother is leaving, i.e., he will cry when she puts on her hat. He begins to see objects clearly as having stable functions and properties of their own and not dependent upon him for existence. For example, an object hidden by a cover is no longer forgotten as soon as it is out of sight. Baby will remove covers to find the disappeared object. In imitating the actions of others, a baby performs actions, such as tongue waggling, which he has already done on his own but which he has never seen himself do.

Stage 5
(12-18 months)
This stage marks the beginning of experimentation. The child begins deliberately to invent new actions he has never tried before and to explore the novel and unique

features of objects. He tries to find what will happen if he uses objects in new ways. He combines objects with other objects to create new ways of doing things. He uses trial and error to discover new solutions to problems.

Stage 6
(18-24 months)
The sensorimotor period ends with the beginning of mental pictures of objects and actions and places in the external world. The child starts to "figure things out in his head" in very crude ways. He still needs the objects present, but he is beginning to build thought symbols for them and these symbols help him to create "new ideas" -- namely, actions that he hasn't seen or practiced before. Space is becoming "filled in" for the child. For example, even though part of the pathway of a ball which has rolled under a sofa is invisible, the baby can now make a mental map of the ball's path and trot around behind the sofa to find his ball. Imitations of some actions of a model are now possible after the model has left. In addition, babies can now begin to play "pretend" games.

Concrete Operations Period, 2-11 years

Preoperational Subperiod
(2-7 years)
The major distinction between a child in the sensorimotor period and one in the preoperational subperiod is that a preoperational child can tell the difference between words and ideas and those happenings or objects to which the words and ideas refer. The sensorimotor child can not. Preoperational children work with words and ideas and manipulate them instead of the happenings or objects they represent. The preoperational child begins to identify a past, present and future. He begins to tell the difference between an action and the plan of action. He forms an image, a "picture in his head," about activities, and he rearranges these "pictures" in preoperational thinking.

Concrete Operations Subperiod
(7-11 years)
Compared to the infant the child is very sophisticated in his thought processes by the time he reaches concrete operations, but compared to the adult he is still not very abstract in his thinking. Actually, he is very concrete-minded in his newly-acquired mental representations of actions and events. Hence the name of this

period and subperiod. During this subperiod the child begins to master many skills. He begins to integrate the various properties of objects, and is less likely to focus on the most obvious property, thereby excluding the others. These skills help him to conserve quantity, weight, volume and number. That is, he now realizes that these properties don't change because of manipulations. He can categorize (put similar things in related groups) and seriate (arrange objects in a regular, special order, such as longest to shortest sticks). He can put himself in the shoes of other people and imagine how things look to them.

Formal Operations Period, 11-14 years

Formal operations "refers to the fact that the adolescent can follow the form of an argument but disregard its specific content. Younger children cannot do that."* Hypothesis building is the task most representative of this period. The adolescent in formal operations abstractly guesses at the ways things might be, and then logically, through memory and/or through concrete actions suggested by his hypothesis, tests out his guess. We see here the final step in the development of thinking. In the sensorimotor period the form of thought was dependent upon the content of experience. In the formal operations period the form of thought selects the content to be experienced.

*Phillips, p. 102.

171

Schema

A schema refers to a variety of actions but also includes the thoughts about the images of actions. Mobility of a schema means that the schema can be applied in a wide variety of circumstances. A young child, for example, can suck on all sorts of objects; he later can use addition and subtraction to solve many different kinds of problems.

Adaptation

To meet new demands a person makes changes in himself and in the world around him so that he can better understand and use himself and the world. The two component parts of adaptation are assimilation and accomodation.

Assimilation

This process brings to the person sights, sounds, etc., from the outside world, and shapes this new information to fit his present understanding and skills.

Accomodation

The process by which a person changes and improves his present skills and knowledge so that he will be able to accomplish new tasks and to understand new information.

Object Concept

The development of the object concept refers to the understanding of the permanence of objects. A child who has the concept of the object acts as if an object which is hidden from sight still exists and hasn't disappeared from the world.

Equilibrium

When a given problem or situation is no longer challenging because a child or adult has learned to deal with or solve all aspects involved, Piaget says that equilibrium has been reached with

equilibrium (cont.)	respect to that situation. As the child acquires more and more schemas which are organized systematically with each other, he becomes equilibrated to a much wider range of such problems or situations.
Symbols	These are abstractions used as labels for objects, ideas and dreams. They are usually private signifiers and bear some resemblance in sound or sight to the object they represent, i.e., a piece of cloth to represent a pillow in a pretended going to sleep action.
Signs	Signs are sophisticated abstractions, i.e., words, numbers, scientific symbols that can be recognized by others as standing for certain objects ideas or concepts. Signs usually do not resemble the objects they represent.
Egocentrism	An inability to see things from another person's viewpoint.
Centration	This is characteristic of preoperation children who pay attention to a single striking feature of an object and neglect other important features.
Decentering	When a child takes into consideration the many aspects and features of a situation or object, he is capable of decentering.
Irreversibility	The child with irreversibility of thinking has an inability to check back over the steps of logic he has taken in order to find out where a mistake might have been made.

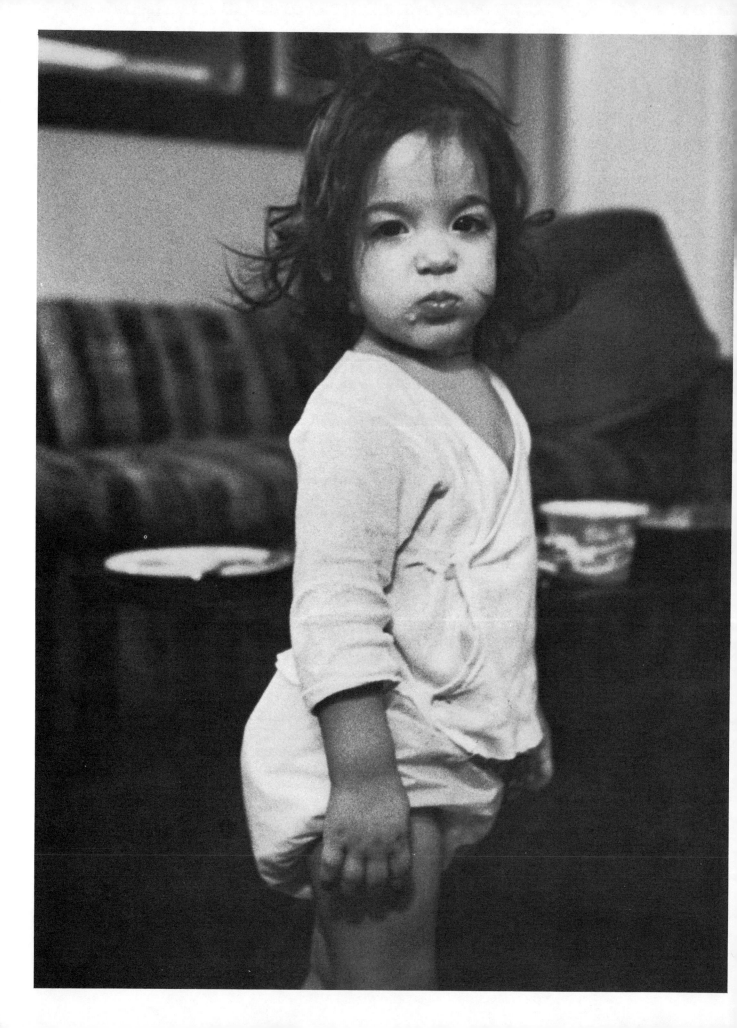

8
USE OF: LIVING SPACE, FURNISHINGS, AND ROUTINES

Before the group meetings begin, spend a morning with your

trainees visiting a few other

preschools. Even though most

preschools visited will be for

older children, the visits --

particularly if you choose a

variety of types of preschools

-- will help the trainees

understand better the inter-

relationship between babies and

their environment.

*E*MPHASIZE THE IMPORTANCE
OF THE PLANNING AND
ARRANGEMENTS OF LIVING
SPACES AS A BASIC PART
OF THE LIFE EXPERIENCES
AVAILABLE TO INFANTS
IN DAY CARE.

Before starting out on your tour of preschools, give the

trainees a list of things to look for. They should be on the

lookout for safety routines or hazards, the uses of space or

storage areas which help children be more sociable or get

toys more easily, and how areas are set up to free children

from distractions so they can work more easily at a task.

After your visits and lunch hour, you may meet together in a

large group to discuss and plan the use and furnishing of Day

Care living spaces for infants.*

*For planning a Day Care environment and furnishings, see:
American Academy of Pediatrics, Chapter VIII, "Facilities
for the Day Care Centers for Children;" Lally, J. R., and
Smith, L., pp. 2-6; Parker, L. K., Huntington, D. S., and
Provence, S., Chapter 3, "Organizing a Child Care Center."

Ask the trainees to think of all the kinds of living areas with which they are familiar. Let them tell you what activities go on in those living spaces or environments. They will probably mention eating in kitchens; sleeping in bedrooms; recreation in game rooms; reading or writing in a study; building in a basement workshop; enjoying grass, flowers or vegetables growing in a garden; playground sports and games; subways or bus stop corners for getting places; closets and chests for belongings; bathrooms for toileting and washing up; living room rugs and couches and tables for sociable parties.

Now ask the trainees for which of these activities babies too need a special space. Ask them, in addition, for activities unique to babies which require special space or furnishings.

Your visits to preschools should give the trainees ideas about different kinds of room and outdoor equipment appropriate for youngsters. Discuss infant living areas in detail. Ask for suggestions as to how such areas can be created. (A large blackboard will be a help to list areas and activities.) If you have toy doll furniture available, ask the trainees to sit in three groups on a rug and try out arrangements of furniture to create or define each living area in turn as it is suggested.

Feeding Space

Large square feeding tables, with safety-strap equipped comfortable infant seats set into them, provide useful feeding

settings for babies. Let your trainees give you reasons why
such tables are to be preferred. They will probably mention
that there is less danger of tipping over such a table compared to a narrow-based high chair, and more room for assorted
dishes or finger foods to be set down. Babies who must wait
for a meal because a caregiver is busy for a moment can be
given these finger foods or toys to play with on a large table
surface. Such tables can be used to seat babies comfortably
for other activities, such as individual soap-solution finger
painting, or for play with puzzle boards. Caregivers will
find the comfortable and adjustable height of such feeding
tables puts no physical strain on an adult seated in front of
the baby who is feeding.

Feeding tables may be lined up several in a row. This makes
feeding of babies easier on a caregiver, and provides a good
opportunity for babies to look each other over and to see
what foods another baby seems to be enjoying. Feeding
tables may be tied together with cord around the legs to form
a kind of wall which can mark off a special play area.

Sinks should be close to the feeding area. Cleanups after
meals are easier, and a baby who is new at the Center will be
less fearful if his caregiver is close at hand.

Toileting Space

Since some of the older toddlers at a Day Care Center will be in early (or advanced) stages of learning to urinate or defecate in a special place, a room for toileting should be part of the Center. Babies are very different in their readiness for such learning; boys sometimes need more time than girls. A special room provided with low toilets or individual potty seats (and a wall storage area for such seats) cuts down on distractions during toileting. However, some toddlers may seem more comfortable with potty use if they see other toddlers on nearby potties. The toileting room can be a sociable place for some infants. A low sink should be available for washing up and for other bathroom activities, such as toothbrushing.

Storage Space

Ask the trainees what they imagine might happen if all available toys and materials were scattered on the floor at all times during the day. They will be sure to tell you that toys with many parts scattered about are not very usable by infants. Babies may lose interest in a toy seen all the time, and find it difficult to <u>choose</u> one toy for himself from such a colorful clutter. Some toys with tiny parts, such as pegs or beads, require a caregiver's supervision since an infant playing with these toys tends to mouth objects a good deal. Such toys need to be placed on high open shelves or in sliding-door storage areas. When toys are above a baby's reach, he can learn to

point to the toy he
wishes. The caregiver
can take it down for
him, name the toy
clearly, and help him
to learn how to call
for his favorite games.
If a child asks for a
new puzzle, his
caregiver should help
him return the puzzle
he has just finished
or tried out before

a new one is given if storage space is used as a learning tool
to teach these rules. Rules for returning toys may be applied
only to small-part games, such as pegboards and puzzles. Toys
such as balls, rattles, xylophones, friction cars or soft
animals should at all times be freely available on shelves at
floor level or at baby's reaching level.

Storage space will be needed for diapers, receiving blankets
and other baby care supplies. Locked cabinets are preferable
for storing powders, lotions, baby food jars and other similar
supplies where safety is a factor. Hallway areas leading into
the Day Care Center rooms may be a good place to put these
closets. Diapers can be stored conveniently on shelves provided
underneath many new models of diaper changers. Nearby storage

plastic cans for soiled diapers should have securely-fitted
tops.

Chests of drawers for extra clothing and for storing special
toys are useful. Long drawers with hand pulls set far apart
are preferable. Can the trainees tell you why these drawers
would be safer than small drawers with easy-to-use pulls when
curious toddlers are about?

Chests are more convenient for the caregiver when the contents
are labeled, such as, "things to hear" drawer, containing jingle
bell wristbands, xylophones, windup clocks, rattles, chimes,
large sea shells and tambourines.

Room Furnishings: For Play, For Privacy

Play Places

A rocking chair or two for a caregiver to feed an infant his
bottle, to soothe him, to read to him, to play language
imitation games, and for other loving and sociable activities,
belongs in every infant room.

Floor pads and rugs are warm places to set babies during their
waking hours. A few toys may be set on these mats in a
semicircle so that a baby stretching his hand or arm can
reach something interesting to feel, grasp, mouth or bang.
Babies can see each other as well as other activities going
on in the room. The infant lying on his stomach or side can

raise and turn his head to look at toys and people.

For older toddlers different types of child-sized stools, chairs and rockers are necessary. Getting one's backside into position for seating and actually sitting down well is a real accomplishment for some 2 year olds. Different kinds of chairs and even a set of two or three steps will give toddlers lots of places to practice sitting. Low tables for puzzles, finger painting and other activities should be available for toddlers. Round tables are preferable to square or rectangular ones with sharp corners. Can the trainees explain why?

A Center needs some private places for toddlers to go when they are not tired or sleepy but feel a need for aloneness or quietness apart from other babies. Ask the trainees to suggest ways one could either arrange room furnishings to provide such privacy places or build them into a room.

Private Places

One wall of a Day Care room may be fitted with cubbyholes or small open closets with a step up from the room to their bottom surface. Each baby may have his own cubbyhole with his name on the inner wall and his photograph or perhaps a picture that he has chosen to mark his cubbyhole wall. Here outer garments can be hung or placed on a shelf near the top of the closet. But here, too, the toddler who comes in one morning after a difficult time at home might want to sit for

a quiet while and just <u>watch</u> other babies who are
busy or noisy. The narrow walls of the cubbyhole
feel protective. Babies who have hectic home lives
need a special private breathing space sometimes
before they feel ready to play in the larger room.

Sturdy, large, colorful cardboard boxes, set side-by-side in an
infant room, mark a barrier between a play area with rug and a
neighboring diapering area, and provide private places for very
young infants. A 10 month old may creep to an open-ended box
and settle for a few minutes of rest and relaxation.

Room furnishings, such as a rocking chair and a large doll bed
against a wall, may serve as resting places where a baby can
feel secure and private for a little while.

Book Places

A reading corner for infants needs special planning. Ask a
couple of trainees to come up and draw on the blackboard some

ideas for helping babies have
colorful books available,
together with comfortable
places to look at those
books, like low-bracketed
shelves on which books are

laid out flat (stools or chairs for reading may be stored under
the shelves and slid out by a toddler who wants to sit and read

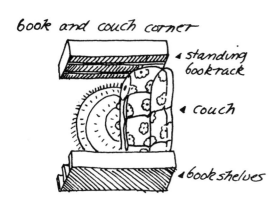

book and couch corner

◄ standing
booktrack

◄ couch

◄ bookshelves

by a bookshelf). Or like a couch and bookcase corner where infants who take a picture book from the reachable shelves can climb up onto a plastic-covered low couch to look at pictures or babble stories to themselves as they point to a page. Such a couch area also allows a caregiver to show picture books to a couple of babies snuggled against her.

An impromptu reading group may consist of three infants in feeding tables in a semicircle around the caregiver's chair. She can show simple picture books and talk about the names of the animals or foods or other items

THE TRAINEE SHOULD BE AWARE OF AND USE THE ENVIRONMENT RATHER THAN UNKNOWINGLY BE CONTROLLED BY IT.

pictured. Each baby can get a turn to feel, touch and name the pictures.

Sleep Space

Very young infants have sleeping and waking patterns which require cribs to be available continuously for one or another infant. For these infants, sleep areas should be partitioned off by doors preferably, or portable screens if necessary, from noisier living areas. Sturdy cribs which double as playpens with nylon net walls are economical and space-saving.

183

Window shades are useful. Older infants may need only one nap a day. For these toddlers low cots which can be stored upright in a locked closet while not in use may serve as beds for naptime. They may be set out by Day Care personnel while infants are at meals prior to napping. A large, cuddly, washable cotton receiving blanket for each cot or crib will make sleep-room settling down easier for infants. The trainees may ask you to provide a low stool so they could sit near a restless baby who needs a back rub or the quiet company of his caregiver before he can drift off to sleep.

Crib And Wall Decor

Cribs and playpens are resting places for tired infants, and are also safe playing spaces for infants needing protective care while a caregiver is busy. Safe toys to swat at or grasp with hands, and mobiles to kick at with feet are important. Mobiles for infants under six weeks should be hung on one side of a crib since a new baby lies with his head turned to one side generally.

Such kick-ables or swat-ables should be familiar to the trainees from prior sessions on sensorimotor coordination games. Can they suggest other living spaces where this equipment can be used effectively? Mobiles may be hung from ceilings or over diapering areas. They serve to _decorate_ a room with color and odd shapes. They serve as interest points for infant glances. Mobiles hanging from ceilings and walls also serve as focal

points for brief hand-exploring visits while the infant is in
a caregiver's arms.

Magazine pictures, large and clear and ethnically relevant to
the infants, make additionally interesting wall decorations.
These may be taped at low furniture levels for viewing by
creeping infants, or higher up on walls near diaper changers
or cribs.

<u>Mirrors</u>

Unbreakable mirrors are available in assorted sizes. If these
are too expensive for your budget, then framed glass mirrors
are safer than unframed ones. Ask the trainees to suggest
places in the Day Care Center where mirrors will be most
useful. They may suggest having mirrors right near diaper
changers so that a baby can see the caregiver's motions as
she changes his diapers and makes him more comfortable. After
being cleaned up, having hair combed or a fresh ribbon put on

hair, a baby can be told, "See
how pretty!" or "Angelo's all
fresh and <u>clean</u>. Look at your
<u>pretty</u> face, honey!" The
caregiver can direct the baby's
eyes to the mirror, or sit the

baby up so he can see himself and enjoy the sight of himself in
the mirror. Mirrors are also useful in cubbyholes where outdoor
clothing is stored. A toddler can appreciate and admire his new

hat or red boots along with the caregiver who has just finished helping him on or off with his clothing.

Mirrors are very important in the special play areas. The trainees will probably mention to you that such mirrors must be hung near floor level and mounted securely so they are safe for babies who may try to pull up to a standing position by the frames.

Mirrors can be placed on a wall or room divider screen where photographs of each infant in the room are taped. A toddler can go to inspect himself in the mirror. Then he can pick out and look at his own picture in a special "See-Yourself Corner." Unbreakable hand mirrors should be available among the infant toys.

Rug-And-Furniture-Defined Play Areas

Ask the trainees: "If a caregiver tries to work at sensori-motor activities on a large open floor space with her four toddlers or creepers, what is likely to happen?" The trainees may smile broadly at their mental image of four creatures padding off in four different directions as a caregiver turns to take down toys from a nearby shelf. Talk about how the babies' physical surroundings can be used to keep them comfortable and

USE FURNITURE TO CREATE NATURAL ENCLOSURES WHICH CAN BE CARPETED AND FURNISHED FOR SPECIAL GAMES AND LESSONS.

and interested while in a given area. Draw on your blackboard some possible uses of furniture, such as chests of drawers or feeding tables, to set up boundaries for such special play areas. Movable sturdy wooden screens may be used for one side of such an

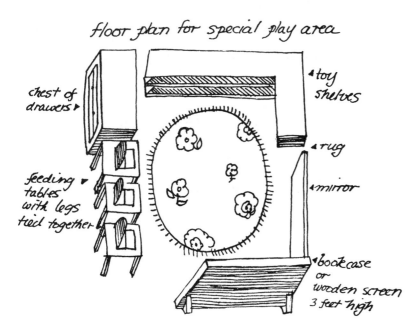

floor plan for special play area

chest of drawers ▸

feeding tables with legs tied together

◂ toy shelves

◂ rug

◂ mirror

◂ bookcase or wooden screen 3 feet high

area if there are too few bookshelves or other furniture available. (Be sure they cannot be pushed over by a baby trying to stand.) Floor level mirrors can be used in these areas to teach body parts, or clothing names, as well as to play peek-a-boo games or to enhance the infant's pleasure at seeing himself.

Taking Advantage Of Other Room Features

Ask the trainees to talk about how they could use room features like window sills, a cork-lined wall, door handles, etc., to increase a baby's interest and pleasure in his environment. Let them make a list of such possible room features which a caregiver could use to provide baby with a variety of sensory and motor experiences.

Keeping Living Spaces And Toys Clean And Safe

The floor rugs used in such areas will need shampooing frequently.
Toys in these special areas, as well as other toys available to
the infants, will need to be cleaned in sudsy solutions and
rinsed thoroughly after a play session during which they have
been lovingly drooled upon, chewed or handled with sticky
fingers. Discuss carefully with trainees the responsibilities
of caregivers for these routines, and demonstrate how one keeps
each part of a living space safe for infants in terms of health
care standards.

Trainees will have to keep a sharp lookout for any sharp corners
or edges of drawers, tables and other furnishings. If some
sharp edges are totally unavoidable, a bumper of old stockings
or mattress-pad material may be taped to that corner. Cheap
disposable paper slippers for caregivers and visitors will keep
floor soiling to a minimum. Spills, runny noses and spit-ups
are frequent in infant rooms, and paper towels, boxes of facial
tissues, and washcloths or squares of soft flannel, are good
supplies to have on hand in abundance for every infant room.
Sliding-door cabinets or tall shelf-tops may be used to store
these cleanup aids.

A Place For Sick Babies

The trainees may be concerned about what their safety
responsibilities are if a baby vomits or feels feverish or

looks listless and pale. Discuss with the trainees these and
other signs of a sick baby. The Day Care Center should have a
place set aside for sick babies who need to be apart from the
other babies for awhile. A good isolating place might be a
small room attached to the Director's office. Let the
trainees decide what furnishings such a room needs. A closet
for medical, diapering and cleansing supplies, a small
examining table, a low cot, a portable crib or crib which
folds out from a wall, are good suggestions for a sick room.
You may want to ask a nurse or pediatrician to visit the
trainees and discuss ways to care for a sick baby until the
doctor arrives or parents can be contacted.

A Space For Living And Growing Creatures

Day Care Centers for preschoolers often have a variety of
nature corners available for enriching the experience and
pleasure of their youngsters. Collections of house plants,
terraria, garden seedlings and bean sprouts on wet blotters
vie for windowsill space. Assorted cold- and warm-blooded
creatures such as turtles, goldfish, hamsters and chicks make
up the miniature menageries of preschools. Sea shells,
leaves, fossil rocks and shed snake skins are some of the
"nature" items which require less tending by staff, but are
fascinating for youngsters to examine with eyes and fingers
and magnifying glass.

Talk over with the trainees what kinds of nature samples they
feel are safe and add visual or sensory delight to a baby's
world. Certainly the life of a goldfish is a hazardous one in
an infant room. Infants left unattended a moment have been
known to plunge their hands eagerly into a fish tank to capture
in a triumphant squeeze one of its golden swimmers. Babies
require clear modeling by a caregiver in such matters as how to

stroke a furry gerbil gently, how to touch a turtle's back
softly, or how to look at and feel the fuzzy leaves of plants
rather than to pluck and nibble them. Still, the joys to be
found from sniffing fragrant daffodils whose bulbs were forced
into winter bloom, or from watching parent gerbils cuddle with
their own bodies the babies they are keeping safe and warm,
are not to be denied to infants. Plants, hanging from wall
planters or reaching toward window light from the sills, make
a nursery gay with greenery.

Using The Day Care Building For Adventures

A Day Care Center, lodged in an old building or church, provides adventurous places and trips for toddlers. Ask the trainees to think of some examples. Stairways can be used for long slow trips up and down, with infants taking one step at a time. Caregivers can make up songs like, *Up the stairs we go; up the stairs we go; hi, ho, the cherrio, up the stairs we go,"* to the tune of, *Farmer in the Dell.*

Visits With Other Infants

Visiting a set of infant rooms belonging to another group is a sociable experience if timed well and coordinated with the caregivers in that group. Inter-group visiting may be made an important part of an infant program where older toddlers are separated from young babies. As the young babies approach the skill levels or age levels which the caregivers and Director see as necessary for moving into an older group, such visits help the growing infant adjust to the new places he will be in the future. His appetite for joining the new group may also be whetted by his chance to see and explore the new toys of greater variety and difficulty which are available to older babies.

Visiting Other Day Care Center Personnel

Holding the caregiver's hand and accompanying her downstairs on a trip for supplies from the kitchen (the source of good foods and snacks) can be a great adventure. The kitchen personnel get a chance to practice caregiving skills in greeting and showing the visiting toddler around the kitchen full of interesting large furnishings: Sinks, dishwashers, counters, cupboards, freezers, refrigerators and stoves.

Visiting Special Center Areas

Some Day Care Centers may have a special small TV room with a rug on which older toddlers can settle comfortably to watch some of the Sesame Street programs, for example. An adult lounge area or a dining area for older infants provide other "trips" for toddlers.

A daily trip to the indoor gymnasium, which Day Care Centers located in northern climates should have, can be the highlight of a morning for infants. Toddlers, whose need for activity seems boundless as they work at getting their newly-acquired skills functioning securely and smoothly, will particularly love the large spaces and freedom a gym provides, along with its treasure-trove of tricycles, climbers, slides, barrels and other large muscle equipment. The trainees should realize that the gym environment has a somewhat different effect on the mood and emotional excitability of the young child. Ask the trainees to suggest ways they can handle too much screaming or yelling or running without squelching the natural exuberance of young children enjoying a gym environment. What ideas can the trainees offer for the end of gym period, when toddlers may need to calm down somewhat in order to leave the gym safely?

Outdoor Worlds To Conquer

An outdoor playground or meadow or small wooded glade may be available to the Day Care Center program. Talk about the use of different outdoor play areas for different activities. Why is it unwise to put a sandbox area attractive to wandering toddlers too close to a swing area? Why should a tricycle-riding area for brave, but possibly wobbly or wild riders be separated from outdoor areas where younger babies may be sunning or creeping about or just sitting and banging shovels and pails together. How can the hard ground at the exit end of a slide be made safe for younger babies? The trainees may suggest that an inflatable air mattress or other mat can be used outdoors to cushion a baby's bottom from the hard ground as he swoops off a slide.

Outdoor water play is a unique summer pleasure for babies. A hose run from a Day Care faucet with lukewarm water can be held still by a caregiver as toddlers dressed only in diapers or training pants run squealing into its wet spray. When an inflatable plastic wading pool is used with young infants, put inside the pool for use by a baby or two seated gently in the pool. A caregiver must be watchful of a baby who does not sit alone steadily for long periods, and stay close to support the baby if necessary. A brief pool experience may be just enough for him. Older toddlers may climb easily in and out of a filled wading pool and heartily splash themselves and each other in pool play.

Stone or hard plastic-molded animal sculptures may be available for babies to "ride" on. A shed where outdoor wheeled toys, inflatable pools, hobby horses, sand toys and other equipment can be stored, is a useful addition to the outdoor area. A toddler can walk into a shed and choose the red trike as the one he wants to ride that afternoon. Watering cans can be stored in a shed for toddlers who want to "give a drink" to flowers planted in flower beds.

For each of these outdoor areas, discuss with the trainees ways in which they can organize and arrange the use of space and equipment so that a few clear safety rules can be set for young children. Such planning on the part of the trainees will cut down on the times a caregiver needs to call out a negative command or to remind or reproach a young child about safety procedures in outdoor play.

9
TOPICS OFTEN FORGOTTEN

Sometime during your training sessions, the prospective infant caregivers with whom you have been working, creating, play-acting and learning will ask you to discuss various topics and problems which they see as needing some discussion and decision-making. Collect as many of these inquiries, doubts, puzzled feelings or factual gaps as you can, and schedule a talkfest on these assorted topics. Some of these topics may not seem to you to be directly relevant to care-giving and infant relations. Many

INSOFAR AS YOU CAN FACE TRAINEE CONCERNS OR QUESTIONS IN PERSONAL AREAS HONESTLY, YOU WILL BE CONTRIBUTING TO THEIR MORE EFFECTIVE SELF-ASSURED ROLE AS INFANT CAREGIVERS.

trainees will ask you to help them solve personal problems. Be sure to discuss any issues which trainees may raise relevant to their work or personal attitudes. Center your discussions on three major potential areas of trainee concern: Interpersonal staff relations, work requirements, contact with parents.

Be candid in stating when your policy decisions are agency-imposed. Where the trainees themselves can act as a decision-making body to formulate rules for handling questions and issues, explore potential decisions with them.

ENCOURAGE ACTIVE TRAINEE PARTICIPATION IN THE DECISION-MAKING PROCESS TOWARD THE CLARIFICATION OF ISSUES.

The trainees may want a clear statement of what personnel carries out what roles. Caregivers may, for example, be totally responsible for all cleanup jobs in the infant rooms. If they use quarters rented during the week from another organization they may be required by the weekend needs of the organization to carry out special take-down-and-put-away jobs every Friday afternoon.

In some Centers there will be special food preparation persons, nurses, clerical personnel or diaper service. In other Centers the caregivers may be responsible for all infant food preparation in their rooms, or for all laundering other than diapers. Trainees have a right to know what jobs they are expected to handle, and a right to training or guidelines on how to handle them. Answer all trainee questions about role requirements. Stress the varied and flexible nature of the caregiving job. Bring in food personnel and the staff pediatrician to speak with the trainees. State clearly who will be responsible for initiating or fulfilling requests for help in the area of food preparation or health care. For example, though a given staff pediatrician may arrange to visit a Center only twice a month, he may teach the trainees how to spot symptoms of sickness. Assign the trainees the task of reporting immediately to the Director any signs of illness which may require a call to the pediatrician.

How Are Babies Assigned To A Caregiver?

In a given Day Care Center the very youngest infants may be
each assigned to a caregiver who will be their special person
for feeding, loving, comforting and learning games. Discuss
with the trainees the implications of such assignments. How
would individual assignments help the caregiver? The trainees
should tell you how much harder it would be for a caregiver
to learn the habits and skills and needs of 20 or even 50
infants in a Day Care Center compared to 3-5 infants for whose
welfare they may be predominantly responsible. Talk about
the particular advantages of this attachment for a baby who
may be mothered by many different persons in his home
environment. Discuss frankly any reservations the trainees
may have about such attachments. Reassure them that such
assignments are not meant to supplant the infant-parent
relation but to supplement it. They are meant to strengthen
the infant's trust in a loving caregiver and to make his
adaptation to Day Care easier. The trainees may ask, "What
if a baby seems to prefer another caregiver or to stop
crying easier if she soothes him?" Stress that the Day Care
Center will be able to make changes and adjust to such events.
The maximum happiness and comfort of the infants is what the
caregivers and the Center are working for.

Trainees may ask, "What if I am sick; who cares for 'my'
babies?" Ask them how they think such problems can be solved.

They may suggest occasional sharing of diapering or feeding tasks with each other so that a baby gets used to care and an occasional assist from another caregiver. These questions should lead naturally to another topic of concern to the trainees: Daily records.

Who Keeps Records? What Kinds Of Records Need To Be Kept?

If trainees will be expected to keep records you must now show them exactly what kinds of information they will be required to provide, when, and where. Demonstrate how to record data. Hand out sample sheets and ask trainees to fill them out as if they concerned real infants of different ages. Have trainees fill out together records for:

Daily attendance

Foods served

Medical information -- for example, vitamin dosage or allergy drops to be administered (and information about rashes or bruises being treated may be useful)

Have the trainees tell you why such records may be helpful to them. They should understand that records for a baby can help a substitute caregiver know more about that baby's food or sleep habits or medical needs. A substitute could then take better care of that baby should the regular caregiver be absent. These records permit a caregiver to be alert to any special changes in growth patterns or habits which might require special attention.

Show the trainees sample sheets for recording a baby's progress
in development, for example, in walking, in solving a means-end
problem, or in imitating an unfamiliar sound. Ask them to
"make up" behavior typical of a baby. Then let them mark down
on your handouts what the baby does according to the notation
or description of these behaviors you have used on the records.
Reassure the trainees that too much paperwork will not be
assigned to them. Care of and attention to the babies is more
important than elaborate records which might keep an adult
from providing this care.

What Are Trainee Responsibilities When They Are Not On The Job?

Get the trainees to formulate with you fair rules about illness,
coffee breaks, unavoidable absence due to personal crisis in a
trainee's family, etc. Each trainee should understand the
reasons for elementary staff rules such as phoning in to notify
the Director in case of illness, not leaving for a coffee break
until you are sure your infants are adequately "covered" by
another caregiver, or being at work on time each day to greet
incoming infants. Center policy for sick leave payment or for
the right to personal crisis time-off-without-pay should be
explained to trainees. A clear statement of these policies
will lessen the possibility of bad feelings among staff members
in relation to each other's sharing in the work to be done.

What Clothes Do We Wear As Caregivers?

Trainees may find they can come to quick decisions that they prefer slacks or shorts for work with infants since they will bend and lift and sit on the floor so often. Other trainees may prefer to wear dresses and smocks. Unless there is some urgent reason involving a particular community's lack of acceptance of such freedom of choice in dress, let the trainees decide individually on what kinds of clothing will be practical and comfortable for them.

How And When Do The Infants Go On Trips Away From The Center?

Let the trainees draw up some reasonable rules for trips away from the Center. A walk around the block with two babies in a double-seated stroller may require only notice to the Director and arrangement with a neighboring worker to care for your other babies while you are gone. A walking trip with toddlers to the local fishmarket or bakery may require advance phoning and planning by the Director and staff. A trip to a local woods or picnic area or airport may require coordination of time and efforts among caregivers, director, parents and Center bus drivers. Assure the trainees that the Day Care Center will support fully their cooperative efforts to plan for and organize such trips for the children.

What Are The Caregivers' Rights And
Responsibilities With Regard To Outsiders?

The trainees may feel that their babies and their program would be disturbed by too many visitors at inopportune times. Ask the trainees to discuss how many visitors would be a "reasonable" number to visit their babies at opportune times during the day. The trainees may want assurances to protect the babies that all visitors be accompanied by a Day Care Staff person or at least wear a visitor's tag. They may decide that visitors be required to remove shoes before entering an infant room. Be sensitive to these trainee suggestions. Praise the trainees for caring enough about the welfare of their infants to raise all these points.

A more special problem may arise if requests are made by local educational institutions to send students to observe the babies and caregivers, or to learn infant care skills by volunteering help to the caregivers, or to measure infants on, for example, Piagetian tasks, developmental achievements or sociability with each other. *Allow the trainees to explore freely their own feelings in response to these situations.* They may welcome volunteers' help or, on the other hand, they may express a preference for observers only since untrained help initially may require too much caregiver time and effort. Ask the trainees: "If you were assured of regular volunteer help at times when you really need extra hands -- such as going-home time, or lunch time -- would you be willing to help teach volunteers some of your caregiving skills?" When volunteers can be viewed by the trainees as potentially helpful personnel to themselves and a good experience for the babies, trainees will be more accepting of "outsiders" in their Day Care rooms.

Discussions of the people who test and their role with the infants may best be handled during in-service training. You can then devote several sessions to explaining different kinds of infant tests currently in use. When the Day Care Center is already in operation, you can offer the trainees demonstrations by testers of some infant achievement tests in the area of language skills or Piagetian concept development. You will be able better to explain what "I.Q." means or answer other questions about infant tests during such in-service sessions.

Firmly reassure the trainees that no person will just come into their room and take infants out for testing without the permission of the Director and caregiver. The trainees may demand of the Director the right to refuse to allow testing on a given day if a baby feels feverish or is upset. Trainees may express an interest in knowing how their babies do on any such testing procedures. Promise to set up conferences between testing personnel and caregivers. At such conferences all questions by caregivers can be answered by the testers in such a way as to be helpful to the persons caring for the infants.

When And How Do We Get Together With Parents?

Make up a list of parent-trainee statements or episodes which would promote either good or poor parent-trainee relations. Have pairs of trainees role-play so that one trainee plays the parent and the other the caregiver. Vary the role-playing situation. Write out episodes where a parent brings a baby to the Center, or comes to call for him at the end of a day, or opens the door to a home visit by the caregiver whose appointment she may further welcome or find inconvenient, or where a parent comes to spend a morning in the Day Care Center.

Vary the kinds of problem situations the trainees will role-play.

A parent visiting the Center tells the caregiver, "This baby is stupid compared to my other kids."

A parent tells a caregiver the Center has done wonders for her baby. The caregiver may be feeling quite concerned because the baby does not seem to respond well to words and verbalizations.

A parent asks the caregiver to give the baby vitamins every day. The parent explains that she forgets and doesn't want to be bothered.

A parent is visiting the Center. She comes in and plays with her baby for only a few minutes. Then she may say, "Goodbye," and wander to other rooms, and leave her baby crying bitterly though the caregiver is trying to comfort the infant.

A parent criticizes the caregiver for not cleaning a baby's chin or hands or bottom as soon as he becomes messy.

Praise trainee dialogue that seems to
restore trust between parent and Center.
Praise trainee dialogue that doesn't
preach at or criticize a parent but
offers specific positive comments to
help a parent find easier or more
appropriate ways to handle his or her
baby's behaviors.

*HAVE THE TRAINEES ROLE
PLAY AS MANY POSITIVE
KINDS OF RESPONSES
AS THEY CAN THINK OF
TO PROMOTE CLOSER
RELATIONS BETWEEN THE
PARENT AND THE DAY
CARE CENTER. ENCOURAGE
THE TRAINEES TO THINK
OF WAYS TO REASSURE A
PARENT OF HIS OR HER
IMPORTANCE TO BABY.*

The trainees may ask you if it will be possible to plan a
monthly potluck family supper where Center staff and parents
can get to know each other better. Accept and discuss other
trainee suggestions for ways to help build a proud and
interested feeling on the part of parents that *This is our
Day Care Center for our children.*

Whom Does A Caregiver See When She Has A Problem?

If caregivers are troubled about a personal problem, or a
problem with another staff member, or a problem concerning
an infant whom they see as not thriving well despite their
efforts, be sure they know to whom they can go. The Center

may be able to obtain access to specialists who are available on call either for personal consultation by trainees or for staff case conferences about a particular baby when necessary.

If you make the lines of communication and referral very clear then trainees will know where and how to go for help with any problems which may arise in the day-to-day functioning of the Day Care Center.

How Do Day Care Center Days Begin And End?

Whether or not the Day Care Center provides busing service for its babies, all Center personnel can help make entering and leaving the Center good experiences for babies. Babies who ride in buses will, of course, be greeted warmly by the driver and attendant rider. Cheerful greetings to baby's mother by bus personnel will reassure the baby of the friendly links between his home and his Center. Go over the safety routines of bus riding carefully with the trainees. Each may at some time be required to help out as a bus rider in an emergency or on a more regular basis. Babies are to be strapped safely into their seats. Simple songs may be sung while the bus makes its pickup rounds. For example, *We are riding in our bus, in our bus, in our bus; we are riding in our bus so early in the morning*, may be sung to the tune of *Here we go 'round the mulberry bush*, while you clap hands in rhythm.

As a new infant enters the bus with the rider, the driver can sing out a greeting like, *Here comes Cassie; good morning, Cassie!* This will help other infants to learn each others' names, though they may belong to different infant groups at the Center. When infants are brought to their rooms -- often three to a driver's arms! -- one may be sleeping, one quiet and bewildered, one already hungry for snack or the breakfast his mother did not find time to prepare for him. The trainees who have become by now sensitive to infants' rights and moods, will be easily able to prescribe <u>different</u> kinds of welcomes, each one warm and sincere, for each baby. Caregivers who genuinely enjoy babies will be able to communicate this pleasure. They will be quick to notice the new hair ribbon or suspenders or shoes with jingle bells and to make a happy comment to each wearer.

Home-going time is a winding-down time. In half-day programs babies may have just had lunch or snack and are ready for home and a long sleep. Caregivers may have to call on special reserves of patience and calm at going-home time. Whether the hat a caregiver puts on baby is indeed **his hat, or whether** his own soiled morning diaper is in the bag being delivered home with him are problems sometimes taken very seriously by parents. If an infant's hat is not double-tied under his chin, he may easily pull open the ribbons. His mother may telephone the caregiver the next day at the Center to protest allowing the baby outside in cold weather with his hat slipped off his ears. Such misunderstandings must be handled with reasonableness and courtesy by a caregiver. Prepare some small "situations" which require tact, explanations and calmness on the part of Center personnel. Have the trainees take part and act out the roles of bus driver, caregiver, parent or other concerned personnel involved in face-to-face or telephone complaints. It is good for the trainees to try to understand the mother's _feelings_ about a hat not on her baby's head, even when they feel the facts are not being considered fairly. Center personnel, through their care, concern and extra patience, can help parents to accept

THE GOAL OF A DAY CARE CENTER IS TO PROMOTE THE FAMILY'S, AS WELL AS THE INFANT'S, WELL-BEING. THE FAMILY PROVIDES AN INFANT WITH HIS FOREVER-SPECIAL PERSONS.

the Center as a place which supports and encourages the family interest in and attention to the baby. Parents may be invited to drop by the Center at going-home time, if possible, to watch the care with which a baby is cleaned, dressed and prepared for going home.

Sometimes an older toddler or baby who comes from a home where too many brothers and sisters are competing for love and attention may find it a wrench to leave a loved caregiver to go home. If a youngster clings to a Center bannister or to a caregiver's arms, he should be stroked and reassured that his special caregiver will be there tomorrow waiting for him. Now it is time for him to go home to his mommy or his daddy or his grandma. If such rare situations do arise during the course of the year, urge the trainees to bring them up in the in-service case conferences or training sessions you will be holding on a regular basis throughout the year. Most of the time a toddler will be ready and willing to "give a kiss" to a caregiver who has given him a warm goodbye hug. He will wave a cheerful "bye-bye" to his caregiver as the driver takes him out to the bus, or as his parent walks out of the Center with him on their way home after an affectionate end-of-day reunion.

10

REVIEW, PLANS FOR IN-SERVICE TRAINING, AND CONCLUSION

In summing up with the trainees the major ideas and feelings gained during the pre-service training program, be very generous with your praise for the good accomplishments of the trainees. A major goal of this last session before the trainees begin their work with infants in the Day Care Center will be to respond warmly to their feelings of competence in caring for and enjoying babies. State honestly your own pleasure at observing some of the specific learning games or loving skills used by trainees with babies during the sessions when guest babies were present.

Divide this last session in two parts. Explain to the trainees that in the first part, you and the trainees will remind each other of some of the important attitudes, facts and ideas you have all been learning and sharing. During the second part of this session, you and the trainees will plan for the in-service training sessions which will be carried out during the coming year.

Section I, What We Have Learned About Infant Caregiving

Frame a series of questions to which the trainees can respond easily. Your questions should help the trainees review the major themes of the pre-service training session just completed.

Development Of Self-Worth

The goals of Day Care for infants include not only education for task performance or competence. It is important to help babies develop self-esteem, trust in human relationships and comfort and joy in living.

Modeling

What we as caregivers really value is what our babies get from us. If by our behaviors we express a genuine pleasure and interest in the world we live in and the persons we live with and work with, then babies will learn from that model. We should model specific behaviors for babies. An adult fixes a broken toy for a baby, comforts the baby who stumbled and fell, waits without offering interfering help as a toddler tries hard to button one button on his sweater. She models mastery behavior, comforting behavior, patient behavior.

Observation Of Development

An adult who is sensitive to where an infant is in his learning and living compared to where she wants him to go in his development can best help the infant to take a new next step onward. Thus, what the caregiver observes and learns

CAREGIVERS LEARN FROM BABIES.

about her baby will often determine how well she can help him to grow happy and competent. A caregiver should learn to observe her own actions and the babies responses to them. She should also be alert to aspects of her room and the materials she can take advantage of in caring better for her infants. She should watch her baby with toys and with other babies to find clues to his styles of play and of exploration.*

Teaching Style

Different caregivers have different life styles. Different teaching styles carried out by genuinely sensitive and skilled caregivers may all work.

Learning By Doing

Babies have to organize their skills and concepts on their own, as well as with a caregiver's help. Adults can't just shovel in knowledge or good feelings or know-how.

LEARNING IS AN ACTIVE PROCESS IN WHICH THE BABY HIMSELF MUST BE INVOLVED.

*A caregiver can ask herself special questions in order to sharpen her observation skills. Here are some examples: "Can this baby recognize people or toys or special places?" "How does this baby cope with strange or new foods or people or toys?" "Does this baby anticipate what is going to happen in a given situation?" "What kind of language ability does this baby have to communicate with people in his world?" "Can this baby recognize simple cause and effect relations in his everyday world?" "What and how have I acted in relation to this baby's actions and experiences in order to help him enjoy or learn from these situations?"

Babies Differ

Babies learn at different rates and in different ways. Caregivers must take individual infant differences and preferences into account.

The Use Of Rewards

Hugs and kisses and smiles and praise when used promptly right after a baby has shown a new and difficult or more mature behavior a caregiver wants to encourage will help increase the chances for that behavior to occur again. How you work with or live with a baby may be more important than what you do with him. A caregiver has to discover the effective rewards for her babies.

CAREGIVERS NEED TO USE POSITIVE REWARDS TO CHANGE BABY'S BEHAVIORS TOWARD MORE MATURE FORMS.

Planning Experiences

A caregiver has to strike a balance between her spontaneous daily activities and those for which she plans. Babies need plenty of free exploration time. They also need adults to arrange special experiences for them to learn or practice certain kinds of skills. For example, a plastic ball with large holes in it makes a good toy for

SPECIAL LEARNING EXPERIENCES CAN BE BUILT INTO EVERYDAY CAREGIVING ROUTINES.

teaching use of the index finger to poke and point. Diapering
time is a fine time for a caregiver and baby to enjoy a good
game of "Where's your nose? Where are your toes?" All these
activities should be planned.

Talking To Babies

Language is an important ingredient in baby's world. A skilled
caregiver talks to her babies. She signals her appreciation of
an infant's early verbalizing despite its garbled quality. She
uses words to go with her own and babies' actions. She also
uses language to express enjoyment of good efforts or actions
by babies. She uses language to break down complicated actions
of a task for a baby. She uses language to offer her babies
alternative ways of doing things.

Support Of The "Parent-Child Relationship"

In relation to parents, the caregiver realizes that her job is
not to take the place of or compete with the child's family.
She is to be a supportive agent to help further a warm
relationship between parent and child. She is to respect
the cultural patterns or bilingual patterns of the infants'
families.

Confident Caregiving

The caregiver whose babies are thriving should see herself as an important person with valuable human skills. A sense of humor

and a lot of patience will be helpful. Some babies may grow

slowly in the ways a caregiver would like. A caregiver with

faith in her own ways with babies will keep on being loving,

friendly and supportive with her baby. And she should be actively

encouraged and supported in turn by her Director!

Section II, In-service Training

Choose, with the trainees' help, a time period which will be set

aside each week for in-service training. The hours between 1:00

and 3:00 p.m. are often convenient. Older infants nap and

volunteers can perhaps be found to help care for younger infants.

Explain to the caregivers that they may feel the need for

further meetings to exchange ideas or information among themselves

and to create new materials for babies. The Director may be

able to arrange for such additional meeting time if she uses the

caregivers of older sleeping infants to help out, for example,

from 1:00 to 3:00 p.m. in the rooms with very young infants.

Other days during these hours the caregivers of the older infants

may meet as a group with one or two of their members accepting

the rotating job of keeping watch in the room with the sleeping

infants. No matter when the sessions take place, in-service

training must be provided for because it is critical to

successful programs.

Talk about where the in-service training or group meetings

should be held. The trainees may want the area to be comfortable like a living room rather than like a classroom. Suggest to the trainees that they appoint a committee among themselves to plan the furnishings of the room or to suggest equipment needs such as a large coffee urn. The trainees may ask you if infant child development materials and books will be available to them in that room on a lending basis. Center funds may permit the creation of a library of resource materials in this room.

Topics For In-service Sessions

Try to have the trainees suggest what they think will be useful or important topics for in-service training sessions. Clarify any topic about which they express uncertainty and make sure you at least cover the following dozen possibilities.

The caregivers will:

Learn special games and songs. Transition times such as preparation for naps or walks from one Center area to another are often more orderly and more fun when special songs or games are routinely used. Staff may demonstrate or role-play for each other "how to" techniques which have worked for them in teaching, for example, circle games like *Ring Around A Rosy* to toddlers.

Hold case conferences on each infant at the Center during the year. Infants who are not thriving well according to a caregiver or who are thriving exceptionally well may be selected for case conference discussions. These discussions will focus on assessing where the baby is situated in major areas of his development and on suggestions for ways to promote his further growth in all areas.

Schedule special lectures by experts. For example, the trainees may want a film and demonstration on mouth-to-mouth resuscitation. They may want a sensitivity-training group leader to conduct a human relations workshop with them to make them more aware of how they relate to other persons -- adults and children.

Learn techniques of behavior management or discipline. Here too, an outside expert in the use of behavior modification techniques may be called in to help plan a program to deal with a particular problem such as a child who hits or bites others with high frequency. The expert can teach the caregivers how to monitor the effectiveness of such techniques when they are used.

Plan for conferences or get-togethers with parents.

Coordinate special in-Center activities by all staff members. For example, if a caregiver wants her children to prepare cupcake batter and then use the kitchen facilities for baking, there will need to be coordination of staff resources and time.

Hear about "What's going on at other infant programs?" Such news may be reported by the Director or interested staff who have read about or visited other programs. This kind of input can give broadened perspective to staff as well as new ideas they may want to try or to modify for use with their own babies in the Center environment.

Create toys and materials to promote specific skills. Caregivers should be provided with a workshop where they can make puzzles and other games for babies. Their ideas about simplified toys which aid a baby in developing fine motor skills can be fully utilized in such regular workshop activity.

Attend refresher sessions on the ideas of Erikson, Piaget or other theorists whose concepts on the development of young children need further explanation. This is a good idea to do after the Day Care Center has been in operation a while. Caregivers will then have more personal experiences to illustrate one or another point made by the theories which are being discussed.

Hold talks to further the Center staff's awareness
and compliance with safety or health procedures.
These talks are necessary from time to time.

Watch films appropriate to infant care. The films
should be analyzed by the group in talks afterward.

Exchange news and views about special events with
the Director and staff. Caregivers may want to
tell about conferences or, for example, local
meetings of NAEYC, which they have attended. The
Director may want to notify the staff on any
funding or policy changes necessary. If a
caregiver has been invited to speak to local groups
about her role or experiences as an infant
caregiver, the whole staff may want to hear about
the event.

Planning The First Month Of In-service Training Meetings

Before you close this session, hand out mimeographed sheets

with several topics and have the group decide on a listing of

dates of the in-service training sessions for the first month.

Part of the first month's sessions can be used by the group

and the person in charge of training to choose the topics

and set up plans for future sessions. Be sure the trainees

understand that future training will depend very much on

their expressions of needs and interests in any given area.

Feedback from staff as to the relevance or clarity of a given

training session is very necessary for further and better

planning to meet the ongoing training needs of all staff

members.

If one is to use the information in this handbook wisely he will remember one important truth. *The child experiences life on many levels at once.* We have provided the reader with information in many areas: Emotional growth, language and reading skills, nutrition, sense experiences, etc. We hope we have enabled the reader to help his trainees to see more sides of the child's life and to understand more completely those experiences essential to healthy development. By looking at one type of behavior at a time a person becomes a more skilled observer. Helping one produce skilled observers was an important task for us. Our chapters were divided by content areas so, for instance, we could talk about emotional development as a separate topic somewhat divorced from other topics. The child, though, is not divided into content areas. He might be reacting to his illness instead of your language lesson, or he might be paying attention to the warmth of your large-muscle game to a greater extent than to the mastery of the large-muscle skill. Children make responses to the total world around them and observe the entire person. They do not see things in compartments.

Our separation of the content areas in this handbook also focuses attention on specific developmental behaviors so that more sensitive, more accurate adult responses to such behaviors could be devised to promote a child's growth. The authors hope that the trainers will be careful "to put the pieces together" as they go through the training program. We stress, in almost every chapter, the connections between the various topics we present. It is the trainer's job to get the future caregivers to see these connections and to help each caregiver to use her new knowledge and skills in a natural way. Understanding of the various topics presented in this handbook is important, but use of this information and other skills in response to the needs and desires of the total child comes with experience, encouragement and additional training. The insightful and enriching experiences that come from this style of communication with children bring the joys and satisfactions of the art of caregiving.

11
SPECIAL TOPICS FOR TRAINING

In this book, we have presented materials that would help the reader understand and nurture the general development of infants and toddlers. This chapter contains information on special topics -- important topics that were not included in the first printing of this book. We hope these topics will be integrated into the training program that you plan. We have found that caregivers trained in these topic areas are better able to meet the child-care needs of the 1980s. This chapter only introduces these topics. Suggested references for a more complete handling are presented for your use in the Bibliography.

This chapter provides child care staff with basic knowledge when program consideration must be given to:

1. Accepting infants under five months of age
2. Communicating better with infants
3. Communicating better with parents
4. Integrating handicapped infants into program
5. Accepting some abused infants into program
6. Infant sexuality
7. Assessment of infant progress
8. Impact of loss or grief experiences for infants.
9. Transitions to preschool from toddler programs
10. Assessment of one's own skills and others' skills as caregivers

The use of role-playing, questioning, discussing trainee ideas, and providing some research evidence (see the Ainsworth and Pines articles, for examples) will enhance topic discussions.

What if You Desire to Accept Babies Under Five Months of Age Into Your Program?

Before infants can creep and crawl, it is important that caregivers carry infants with them during daily activities. When a child cannot move on his or her own to reach a desired caregiver or to come in contact with new sensory experiences, then both emotional and intellectual development are affected. While the child is in the womb, a natural experience of movement and touch is constantly available. Once out in the world the infant must depend on others for sounds, movements, and feelings of closeness. The very young baby has a limited understanding of time, but a body understanding of what feels good and secure -- the arms and lap of the caregiver. Not able to move to gratification and unable to gauge how long he or she has been or will be without gratification, the infant experiences intense distress until gratified and intense pleasure once gratified. As a sense of time develops, hope gradually develops -- hope that one's environment will continue to make things right by providing what feels good and by returning one to a safe and pleasurable state.

Erik Erikson speaks of the early experiences of the infant as opportunities for the infant to develop a sense of trust or mistrust. The early experience of having one's subliminal needs met helps to form a sense of trust. A child moves into the second half of the first year of life somewhere along a relaxed/anxious continuum. Based on early experiences, children develop expectations about how they will be treated in the world, along with early subconscious decisions about their own lovability. A child has learned how much he or she can trust that the principal caregivers, the larger environment, and the child's own body will provide security. Caregivers can positively influence children's early expectations by providing a sense of well-being. This can by done partly by:

1. Quickly picking up infants when they cry;

2. Holding infants close to you and allowing them to experience your warmth and heartbeat, touch large portions of your body, and feel the protection of your arms;

3. Using a sling with four-, five-, and six-month-old children to support their weight and keep them in contact with you;

4. Nursing and feeding young infants in your arms;

5. Allowing the child to begin naps in contact with you.

A sense of well-being is not all the caregiver will provide through caregiving and closeness. The caregiver will also provide a learning base from which the infant can safely explore the world. Safe in the arms of their caregivers, infants can confidently explore sensory and movement displays before them. Not anxious about well-being, infants can give free reign to their sense of wonder. And once they are mobile, many new sights, sounds, touches, and temperatures will be available to them. Some of the lessons learned include familiarity with distance and space relationships, crude classifications of objects and people, and visual perspectives from various positions (front, back, under, over). The infant can explore and experience different voices, facial expressions, and body types as well as feel the varying body tensions and relaxations of the caregiver as he or she interacts with other humans.

Finally, movement itself is enriching. Holding an infant to

shoulder promotes alert looking. When combined with human contact,
movement further enhances emotional security. Cross-cultural studies
show precocious motor ability and enhanced sociability in infants with
unlimited access to caregiver bodies. Therefore, during the first
six to eight months of life, the time before infants creep and crawl
and explore on their own, it is particularly important that caregivers
carry infants with them often and provide infants with the sensations
of skin-to-skin touch and movement.

What if You Desire to Communicate Better with Infants?

There are many ways to communicate with infants. Talking is only one
way. Attachment and sensitivity to infant signals are two other
important ingredients for good communications. "Attachment" is the
term used to describe the special bond of love between an infant and
a loving and loved caregiver. Infants show attachment when they
smile, call out to, chuckle for, maintain eye contact with, nuzzle,
move toward, reach for, and caress a caregiver. They reveal
attachment by exhibiting distress when a loved caregiver leaves the
room and by accepting comfort from him or her upon return. They show
attachment by being willing to move off and explore the environment
if a loved caregiver is available in sight. Attachment allows babies
to explore courageously, allows them freedom to learn and to take
risks. Loving leads to learning. Loving leads to cooperation with
the teaching one. See if your infants communicate attachment.

To communicate better with infants, be responsive to babies'
basic needs for feeding, clean diapers, sleep, position change, and
body loving.

Learn to read infant signals. Observation skills will help

caregivers notice when babies have needs and how babies respond to adult efforts to meet those needs.

Spend time offering interesting stimulations in judicious doses to babies. Get your cues about what is judicious from the baby.

Arrange toys and activities so that infants can learn on their own. Intellectual development is generated by explorations and discoveries initiated by the child who struggles to make sense of his or her discoveries. Caregivers best promote this learning when they provide just enough challenge, just enough newness to entice active infant exploration, infant construction of new knowledge, and infant problem-solving.

Talk a lot with babies. Talk about what you are doing. Repeat infants' sounds. Talk about what they are doing or handling or feeling. Sing to babies. Point out pictures to them and tell them stories in words about pictures. Encourage understanding of both verbal messages and expressive language. All these activities help infants learn language.

Make sure that rules of behavior in the nursery are clear and consistent. Removal from situations where the toddler has behaved unacceptably (hit another, for example) should be done firmly and promptly. Communicate rules empathetically. Research shows that when adults explain earnestly how distressed they are if their infant gives sorrow, pain, or discomfort to another, then toddler altruism increases (Pines 1979). Parents who are frequently loving and who frequently explain the consequences of hurtful behavior on victims have babies who try more frequently to make reparations. Show that hurting is unacceptable. Give pleasure with kisses, with caresses. Show delight in baby hugs and love offerings.

As caregivers show emotional good will for infant attempts,

learning struggles, body features, personality, and abilities, then babies will develop self-confidence. Communicate through your words and actions that you expect babies to be lovable.

A caregiver's expressed pleasure and interest in interacting with infants is the surest guarantee that good attachment and good communication will be built between adult and child. Watch for messages from infants.

Be aware that infants have the need to be close but also the need to be on their own, doing their own touching, building, arranging, squishing, and discovering. This ebb and flow between "oneness" and "separateness" (see Kaplan 1978) is characteristic of infants. Caregivers need to communicate their acceptance of these tendencies that characterize toddlers particularly.

Spend time with trainees discussing when not to interfere in toddler learnings. Turning a shape box so the infant can just push a square block successfully in the hole does <u>little</u> for learning. Offering a shape box with choices and letting the infant struggle to match a few blocks to the shaped holes is far more enriching developmentally. Arranging for learning experiences is an important function of a quality caregiver.

Talk to babies so they know that a caregiver knows what they are feeling. Share the following anecdote with trainees and have them discuss what principles of communication were involved in handling this situation.

In a pediatric clinic cubicle a toddler was having his ears cleaned out by a nurse. As she probed with a Q-tip she kept reassuring the youngster that "this won't hurt at all." The toddler cried and squirmed hard. Mother, holding the tot on her lap, picked up the nurse's words: "It doesn't hurt. If you don't hold still and quiet down I'm going to spank you." Threats and reassurances didn't work. Crying turned to hollering and screaming. Adult threats redoubled. Another staff member approached the youngster quietly and said quite firmly, directly, and calmly to the child, "You really feel scared when someone is poking around in your ear. That feels so scary." The child looked up, stopped crying rather suddenly, and affirmed, "Yeah, I was scared. I was scared!"

What if You Desire to Communicate Better with Parents?

Just as caregivers need to respect the unique personhood of each infant they serve, so must parents be accepted and respected as persons. Most parents care deeply for their child's welfare and well-being. Yet, some parents are needy people. They themselves may not have been given enough loving when they were younger. They may not be so ready to give of themselves, to nurture small children. Immature parents and teenage parents may still need parenting themselves. If a program has a social worker or outreach parent involvement workers on staff, they may be able to help provide supports for parents. Where an infant fails to thrive, such supports may be urgently necessary and require trained personnel (see Fraiberg, Adelson, and Shapiro 1975).

But suppose caregivers are working in a group care situation where there are no special staff to support parents. Then drop-off and pick-up times need to become times to communicate and share with parents.

Parents and caregivers are partners. Yet sometimes a parent feels that a caregiver is more skilled. Baby bursts into tears when the parent comes to pick up the child. "Oh he never cries like that during the day," a caregiver may blurt out. A caregiver needs to convey to a parent the meaning of an infant's fussing or disturbance, such as: "He got so excited just seeing you that he burst into tears. You are so important to your baby. He missed you so much." Or: "He is so emotionally close and attached to you. That is why he can let go in front of you. That is a good sign. Well-attached babies are able to learn better. Babies need that kind of intimate caring and bonding to have the courage to explore and find out about the world in which they are growing up."

A single mother of twins reported, "My girls tear up books when I get them home after 9-10 hours in day care. I have to spank them and punish them. They are never so naughty in day care."

If we punish infants for acting out strong emotions that spill over when they are finally with us again after a long day's absence, what are babies learning? They learn that the excitement from emotional closeness cannot be managed well. It is punished. They learn that getting too close in feelings has dangerous consequences. Trainees need to explore these important ideas through personal discussion.

Caregivers supplement but do not supplant parents. Quality caregiving provides peace of mind for parents. Quality caregivers send messages that promote a close bond between parent and child: "I just love the way his eyes light up when you come to pick him up." "She just wraps her arms around you to let you know you're the most special person in the world." "She can run off to play with her friends so easily when you drop her off. She really feels so secure and well-loved that she can adjust easily to day care." "She really needs you to stay a while each day until she gets used to the nursery. You and her home are so familiar to her. Here everything is new and strange. You are such a help to her when you stay a while. You help her gather more and more courage until she will feel comfortable enough to be without you for a longer while here. Your patience with her adjustment period is a real gift to her."

Teach trainees communication skills. Ask caregivers to suggest ways that they can build a community of concern: caregivers and parents working together to promote optimal development. If necessary, add these to the suggestions offered by trainees:

1. A "memo to parent" can be safety-pinned to each infant's outer clothing if babies are bused. The daily note can record small ventures and victories, new interests and friendships, new foods tried, new skills begun, new ideas glimpsed.

2. A bulletin board or large ledger book at the day care entry can be used to exchange concerns. A parent notes such concerns as when an infant has not slept well or perhaps has vomited during the night. A caregiver can write a message for parents to read at going-home time. Caregiver messages, if possible, should be brief, informative, and supportive.

3. Personal contacts and conferences with parents require ingenuity and planning. Parents may come to meetings if there is someone available to care for children, if food is served, if slides of their infants will be shown, if toys or activities are demonstrated, if they feel their troubles or concerns will be considered empathetically and helpful counsel may be available during parent sessions, and if there is opportunity to meet with and share with other parents socially. A saw and sewing machine, a coffee machine, a crafts center, provide opportunities for parents to meet their own adult social needs to meet and possibly work together.

4. Toy-making and provision for infant development learning may

depend on parents first feeling that their personal-social needs have been addressed. Parents are the first teachers, the most loved teachers of their infants. Provide needed equipment and know-how to carry out learning games at home. Toys can be lent out from a toy lending library. Communicate your understanding that the learning process is <u>child</u> initiated as well as adult enticed, so parents can have success experiences with their children.

5. Talk with trainees about why some parents are uncomfortable about expressing love. Were they punished excessively or denigrated as children? Negative messages they send may be the only messages they know how to communicate. Share your knowledge of what infants and children need.

6. One important thing we know they need is to be loved and to feel that their lives are worthwhile. There is a difference between <u>being</u> loved and <u>feeling</u> loved. An infant needs to <u>feel</u> loved. Parents can communicate this verbally by saying "I love you." They can act affectionately and give warm smiles, hugs, kisses, and cuddles. Research shows that the more promptly parents meet a crying baby's needs, the less a baby will cry by the end of the first year of life and the more compliant the baby will be (Ainsworth 1977).

7. Have caregivers act out how they can provide ideas and ways for parents to encourage little caring acts and kindnesses from their infants. A baby may want to share a biscuit with Daddy. Baby may share his Teddy or blanket when Mama has a headache or feels tired. Letting toddlers help in household tasks contributes to feelings of being worthwhile and important in the family.

8. Talk with caregivers about casual tips and information that can be shared with parents while preparing youngsters to go home. An infant needs language enrichment. Caregivers can suggest using time

while doing dishes, chores, or housecleaning to talk with baby. If a parent uses "no-no" a lot while with an infant, a caregiver might point out gently and calmly that too many "no-no's" can confuse and discourage an infant. Such an infant may even drop food to the floor and call out "no-no" while so doing, as if that word is the name of the game!

9. Parent-caregiver conferences and informal contact times can be used to talk about a child's self-concept. Self-concept depends on how parents and family and caregivers perceive, view, and respond to the infant. Phrases like "you are so clumsy," "you're stupid," and "you're a bad baby" teach children to think of themselves as "dumb" or "no good."

10. Caregivers who build good rapport with parents may want to keep a list of questions for parents which can prod them into thinking about home supports or obstacles to the development of good self-concept. Encourage trainees to think of such questions. Examples: How does the child feel about her or his body? Does the child constantly seem to need praise or reassurance? How does the infant cope with failure, frustration, accidents, or mistakes? Trainees should discuss frankly what kinds of parent answers might influence more negative or more positive self-concepts in young ones.

The gift of a good self-concept is priceless. This lavish gift permits a child to grow up feeling competent and kind, cooperative and sociable, communicative and capable. Help trainees see how their relationship with parents and the ways that they treat the parents can help nourish infant self-concept. Parents need encouraging words from caregivers.

What if You Decide to Integrate
Handicapped Infants into Your Program?

Caregiver beliefs. Caregiver beliefs about handicapped babies can facilitate or hinder the optimal progress of the infants. Consider with caregivers three important beliefs that will optimize mainstreaming efforts.

1. Infants have needs which are to be considered first. In addition, handicapped infants have special needs related to their disabilities. But the special need is only part of what defines the handicapped infant and is certainly not the part that concerns the infant's development the most. Full developmental needs are too often neglected in programs that primarily focus on the disability.

All infants need lots of cuddling and affectionate pats. An infant who lags motorically in steadying his or her head may need to be held so that the head is better supported. But cuddling is just as necessary and nourishing as for normal infants.

Sometimes the caregiver conveys excessive anxiety to a disabled infant or views the infant primarily as a disabled individual. Then interactions with that infant may adversely affect the infant's development of confidence, trust in self and in others, initiative, and independence.

2. Disabled infants need activities and experiences that are interesting and exciting to them as much as do nondisabled infants. Family and staff that focus exclusively on skill training to deal with disabilities, without adequate attention to joyful and interesting experiences, can create a grim first few years of life for their infant. Unnecessary restrictions placed on disabled infants can limit their opportunities for the kind of exploration and discovery that supports development.

234

Caregivers will need to devise and implement learning experiences that promote interest and joy. Bower (1977) has reported work with a blind baby who lay expressionless and inactive. A mobile was devised that provided interesting sounds as feedback every time the baby kicked the mobile. Not only did the baby work hard to keep the mobile in motion, but his face became animated. He burst forth with smiles and coos. Discovering the ramifications of the "kick-to-make-the-sound-happen" game was a joyful experience. Learning gave the baby pleasure.

Emphasize what babies can do and can learn. Arrange successful experiences. Assist the child in doing well in at least one area.

3. The emotional style that an adult uses in interaction with an infant teaches the infant much about how to view and be viewed in the world.

Infants gain social and emotional messages from the styles used by caregivers while performing a task. If the caregiver is required to do special exercises or therapy with a handicapped toddler, how the adult expresses caring and encouragement as he or she carries out the special exercises will make a real difference to the child's emotional and social well-being.

Sometimes caregivers detract from a baby's initiative by doing too much for the handicapped infant. A language-delayed toddler needs a chance to ask for rather than point to a cookie or milk or more juice even if just the initial sounds are produced.

If toys are always placed in a blind or motorically delayed baby's hands, the baby has little motivation to reach or stretch or crawl a bit for a nearby toy. The caregiver can squeak the toy or jingle it to lure the baby. Babies have an internal drive to learn about and make sense of their world. Caregivers can mobilize and challenge this intense motivation.

Skill training. Skill training related to a handicap should of course be considered a vital part of any program. But such training should be placed in the perspective of the larger purpose of creating rewarding environmental encounters for infants.

Be sure that the trainees grasp the concept that an essential requirement for an excellent program is that those who work with the infants view those infants first as individuals with infant needs and additionally but secondly as individuals with special needs.

How does this work out in child care? Give an example and see if trainees can give others. For example, a motorically handicapped baby may be draped over a large play ball in order to increase muscle tone or promote postural adjustments. Let this skill training activity become the vehicle for exploratory learning rather than just focusing on positioning the infant on the ball. Arrange for an attractive toy to be placed close by so that, thus positioned, the baby can stretch out to reach the alluring object. The aim of this activity then becomes a Piagetian means and ends game appropriate for the infant, rather than the narrower aim of muscular therapy only.

Help with hands. Some special considerations may be necessary in working with handicapped infants. Discuss with trainees situations where hands-on help may be needed to assist a handicapped infant to perform a task. Unobtrusive help is especially useful. Trainees can practice putting their hands on another's hands to help steady an activity such as seating a jointed small doll in a toy chair. Caregivers can become adept at manually guiding rather than doing things for disabled infants. Let the infant try as much of a task as possible. Careful matchmaking and sensitivity to the infant's level of interest and ability will aid trainees to increase their assisting in but not domination of the activity. For an infant with motor problems, verbalizations should accompany manual guidance whenever possible.

Model how to. Another difficulty may arise as trainees realize that some slow-to-learn babies may often need a caregiver to show them how yet not to take away the learning curiosity that impels explorations. In some learning situations, slow clear modeling by a caring adult provides an important assist for a developmentally delayed infant. Some programs integrate older retarded toddlers with younger normal infants. The latter provide models of more age-appropriate language and problem-solving behaviors for the special children.

Focus attention. Many developmentally delayed infants need strong stimulation to help them focus on a task. Before modeling can be successful, some infants will have to be helped to focus on persons, materials, and tasks. Caregivers will need to use enthusiastic, dramatic words and gestures. Broad smiles and cheers, handclaps and hugs, help the inert infant become aroused and alert to the game. Verbal praise and strong demonstrations of affectionate encouragement for eye contact and for body orientation to the activity may be required before basic focus on a game can begin. Enthusiastic stimulation, but not overstimulation, can provoke orientation to intriguing materials. The babies can then learn on their own through examination and manipulations. Caregivers need to sit close to a toddler and say "look at me," and, for example, show a baby how to clap two blocks together. Once they arouse the baby to try a game, then the baby receives sufficient feedback and interest from actions on materials to keep the game going.

Arrange the environment. Challenge trainees to think of ways that they may need to rearrange the environment so that infants with various handicaps can have experiences with grasping, squeezing, steadying, pouring, etc. Ingenuity may be needed to facilitate skill building and opportunities for exploration. In all curricular arrangements, caregivers will need to focus on creating stimulating environmental encounters so that infants and toddlers with special needs can also experience the excitement and pleasure of exploration and discovery. Multiply physically handicapped toddlers can have braces removed and be allowed to slither and explore toys and each other safely on a large, bean-bag surface.

A blind toddler can be offered sand to feel and water to swish hands through while a caregiver reads a story about a child at the beach.

A toddler who can neither sit nor walk may be strapped to a special tilted board. Such a board can enable the child to feed him or herself from a food tray placed on a shelf where the board comes to rest. Discuss with trainees the cooperative teamwork with specialists that may be necessary to implement such arrangements.

What if You Decide to Accept Abused Infants into Your Program?

Abused babies enter programs with grave risks for failure to develop normal loving and learning skills. Share research findings with trainees (George and Main 1979). Abused toddlers more frequently threaten or physically assault peers and caregivers. They more often avoid or act ambivalent about friendly adult overtures in comparison to normal toddlers from families under stress. Rarely does the abused toddler simply turn to look at a caregiver making a friendly overture.

Damage to basic psychological trust as well as to their physical bodies may be severe in neglected or abused infants and toddlers. Discuss with trainees how they could offer warmth and body availability without pushiness.

Caregivers cannot allow abused infants to strike or hurt them. They must control the striking hand and firmly give I-messages: "I cannot let you hurt me. I do not want to be hit." Yet, whenever possible, caregivers must model caressing, stroking, loving motions with the child's hands and by their own gestures. Quick caregiver response can halt an infant's blow.

Explain how an animated continued focus on a task may allow continued involvement of caregiver and infant in solving a puzzle or perusing a picture book together.

Discuss the concept of the "Magic Triangle" -- of adult, child, and materials. When caregivers focus the infant on the activity or game, rather than on the persons, the infant often will become more personally comfortable.

Giving attention continuously to inappropriate assaultive attempts may even increase an abused infant's actions. Firm non-acceptance of aggression coupled with a great deal of loving interaction focussed on tasks can increase a baby's chance to respond appropriately. Building trust with normal infants takes time. Building trust where initial trust has been violated and damaged and where hurt is expected from adults takes far longer.

Challenge caregivers to reflect upon their own responses to an abused child's violence. Caregivers need to monitor their feelings honestly. Will they tend to avoid the abused infant who is not gratifying to approach, who does not respond happily to positive overtures? Do adults tend to overlook scape-goating of or bullying by an abused infant because they feel frustrated, unsure, or too busy?

Abused infants need to be swaddled in love, lured by love, but not forced to look at or respond to the adults. As they grow to trust adult caring and firm fairness, abused infants may gradually decrease hurtful and avoidant behavior and increase appropriate responses.

Caregivers need to guard against playing the role of the angry punitive parent, the only interaction with which the infant is comfortable or familiar. New ways of reciprocal pleasing and cooperative sharing in games and in care routines must seem alien, even frightening at first. Prescription for change involves persistent provision of bodily security and comfort and interesting, intimate games, along with consistent refusal to allow aggressive acts.

Discuss the following variables with trainees:

1. Direction of focus of the infant on materials, peers, adults;

2. Comfortable distance for infant from unfamiliar and familiar persons;

3. Time that the infant needs to become comfortable in order to orient, touch, and to allow self to be touched or held;

4. Degree of unfamiliarity of caregiver (i.e. how close in appearance and personal style to parents).

Explore with trainees how these four variables need to be kept in mind as caregivers strive toward normalizing an abused infant's relationship with materials and persons.

What Do You Need to Know about Infant Sexuality?

Have trainers write down questions they want to know about infant sexuality. Include the following ideas in answering these questions.

Babies are sensual beings. They respond with wriggling pleasure to hands that caress their bodies, voices that coo lovingly into their ears, eyes that smile delight and love. Babies explore their bodies. A thumb or fist is brought over and over again to the mouth. Baby's hand catches at a raised foot and clutches the toes. So too will infants discover the pleasurable sensations they feel when they touch their genitals. Feeling their sexual parts is a natural action of infants. Sometimes a toddler will even confide trustingly to a caregiver, "This is my best-feeling part," as she pats her vulva or rubs her clitoris.

A little boy may manipulate his penis which erects slightly and then watch interestedly as he wiggles it up and down. Caregivers who accept occasional sexual feelings and sexual pats or rubs as a normal part of development will help infants and toddlers feel normal about their early sexual discoveries and activities.

What should a caregiver do if a toddler enters day care with a strong habit of clutching his penis and sucking his thumb? Some toddlers use self-stimulation to gain security. They rock back and forth, clutch themselves, suck a thumb, and try to tune out people or program activities. An upset infant needs a calm caregiver. Accept a baby as she or he comes into the program. As caregivers build a secure, trusting relationship, gradually an infant becomes reassured. The world is loving, predictable, safe. Hands that clutched will now begin to reach out to play with toys, to hug people. The compulsive self-comforting through constant body-touching will diminish. Shaming a child or constantly telling a child "no, don't do that" are adult responses guaranteed to inhibit the growth of trust, affection, and infant self-confidence. A good deal of self-stimulation is a signal to an observant caregiver. This child needs more loving from adults. This child feels somewhat insecure and troubled.

Should toddlers toilet together? Toddlers who have experienced toileting together with children of both sexes will feel more comfortable and easy about how a boy looks and how a girl looks. When young children are deliberately kept from seeing each other, then in preschool they may be shocked and highly upset to discover, as one four-year-old exclaimed in great distress on seeing a preschool girl toileting, "She doesn't have a wee-wee!" Early experiences with undressing, dressing, and toileting in a nonsegregated setting create a comfortable climate of acceptance of differences. Caregiver attitudes, caregiver calmness, and matter-of-fact simple acknowledgment of sexual parts and sexual differences will help children grow up more accepting and comfortable with human sexual differences.

Little children sometimes exhibit their genitals and excretory areas. They may pull down pants and laughingly show their "behind hole" to someone. They are just as likely to show their newly polished fingernails or freshly cleaned teeth. A caregiver can restate a rule calmly, "Please pull up your pants, Brenda. We pull our pants down when we go to the toilet. We are not in the bathroom. Pants up, please."

Opportunities for infant nakedness may be available in some

programs in warm climates. Outdoor water spray or pool play on a hot day may provide a chance for infants to enjoy splashing while naked or perhaps while clothed only in diapers.

Sex role identification and how it develops. In the dress-up corner of a playroom toddlers will sometimes put on clothing conventionally used by adults of the other sex. A boy may slip into a pair of high-heeled shoes. A girl may put on a man's hat or tie. If a parent or caregiver expresses anxious dismay at such dressing up, then children may redouble these behaviors in order to keep that extra adult attention focussed on them.

An infant who has ample opportunity to interact with male and female adults who are comfortable with their own sexuality and sex-role identity will ultimately choose to become like the loved caregiver of the same sex. Excessive worry or disapproval of a little boy's nurturing a doll, for example, or of his carrying a pocketbook in play, will only lead to his feeling vaguely wrong and bad and uncomfortable about his choices. Caregivers who slap or threaten a male infant for playing with dolls because they imagine that such play could lead to homosexuality later in life are ensuring that their confusing messages will heighten sex-role anxiety rather than avoid trouble. Furtive sexual explorations, tense gigglings, denigration of others' sexual parts -- these can be the preschool legacy of infants if caregivers are not calm and truthful about bodily functions.

Sexual intrusions. Suppose a child tries to undress another child or poke foreign objects into body orifices of another toddler? Some children grow up in chaotic circumstances. They see adults blending cruelty with sexual overtures. They get the message that bodies are forbidden, dirty, and exciting. Do not permit any child to interfere with the bodily freedom of another. Do not allow a toddler to coerce another into furtive bodily acts. These rules must be clear-cut in order for unambiguous messages about body rights to privacy to be communicated by group care personnel. Yet caregivers must also be careful not to misinterpret body acts of toddlers. A toddler went over and carefully lifted the dress of a little girl. Then he touched her belly-button with grave wonder and satisfaction. Caregivers need to be careful not to impute sexual motives to children who are at times simply curious about each other as people, not as genital beings.

What should caregivers do about dirty words? Some children come from homes where violent and hurtful words are used in anger. At the end of the infancy period, some toddlers may bring scatological words into a group care program. A toddler who, for example, angrily calls another child a "fucker" needs to have rules of address firmly stated: "Each child in our day care center has a name. His name is Steven. Steven wants to be called by his name. And I will make sure that we call you by your name too, Danny. If you are angry, tell us in words what you are angry about. Then we will be able to understand what you need."

Excessive attention to bad words will heighten a young child's interest in these words. A caregiver who has been using "please" and "thank you" and loving tones and words with infants and toddlers provides a model of kind words and affectionate names for children. Calm responses rather than disgust with bodily functions plus loving body cuddling and comforting when a child needs these will do more to ensure positive sexual attitudes than any lecturing or scolding of

244

young children. Each person deserves bodily privacy. Privacy does
not mean that intimate body parts are disgusting or bad. They are
just private. Tender hands and voices that communicate matter-of-fact
acceptance of bodies and bodily functions while diapering, cleaning,
bathing, or dressing will go far toward favoring healthy sexual
development in infants and toddlers.

What Do You Need to Know about the Screening and Assessment of Infants?

Screening measures such as the Denver Developmental Screening Test
(DDST) give a rough idea of whether or not a baby is developing
normally or needs extra remedial help to prevent possible
developmental delays.

Caregivers can learn to use a screening test such as the DDST
in a few hours of explanations and practice. If the DDST suggests
that an infant is performing below chronological age level on two or
more items in two or more developmental areas (language, gross motor,
social, fine motor), then caregivers are alerted to the need for
further diagnostic assessment.

The infant developmental tests that are used for more detailed
diagnosis require a trained examiner. Trained examiners should be
thoroughly familiar with infant tests and with ways to engage babies'
interest and involvement with materials so that a true measure of
infant ability is obtained. Some infant tests available are: Bayley
Scales of Mental and Motor Development (Bayley Behavior Record),
Cattell Infant Intelligence Scale, Griffiths Scale of Infant
Development, Gessell Developmental Schedules, Casati and Lezine Stages
of Sensorimotor Intelligence in the Child from Birth to Two Years,

and Uzgiris and Hunt Ordinal Scales of Psychological Development.

Caregivers should talk with parents if screening test results suggest concern for an infant's development. Nationally, the Child Find program has made it possible for parents to seek expert help for assessing the development of young children at risk. Parents must be included in the assessment procedures. They play an active role with professionals in deciding to seek out special or remedial services.

Remember that testing instruments do not dictate a curriculum. They just tell us about infant strengths and weaknesses. Very often caregivers fall into the trap of training infants so they can pass their tests. This leads to narrow and rigid interactions. Create diverse learning environments for children to attain new skills. Remember how they learn, not how they test.

What Do You Need to Know about the Impact of Loss and Frightening Experiences for Infants and Toddlers?

René Spitz was an analytic physician whose film "Grief: A Peril in Infancy" can be useful in training caregivers for sensitivity to infant reactions to loss. This film shows poignantly the massive sorrow that an infant feels and expresses when deprived of the close attachment to the mothering one. Formerly bright-eyed babies whose mothers were forced to leave them for several months became listless, dreary-eyed, and frightened. Bounce and bloom disappeared. The children no longer seemed to care to learn. Strangers' arms offered a bit of comfort, but when the stranger left, grief and wailing redoubled in intensity. Disinterest in surroundings was marked.

If a baby in group care has just suffered the loss of a beloved parent, whether temporarily (as in a parent's hospitalization) or forever (as when death or desertion occurs), caregivers must be alert to reactions of massive bodily distress. The infant may show disturbances in sleep and in feeding. Sickness, bowel irregularity, inconsolable crying, and apathy may ensue. Conferences with the remaining parent or guardian are advisable. The caregiver to whom the baby is assigned in group care needs to give particular loving and body nurturance. If loss of the beloved parent figure does not last long, or if a substitute parenting figure can be found, the baby will gradually emerge from the disturbance and despair triggered by the loss. Where substitute mothering care is unavailable, there is a serious possibility of later depression.

Frightening experiences, such as a temporary hospitalization or brutalization can also cause severe upset in bodily functioning. Day care setting personnel on split-shift need to coordinate planning so that a stressed youngster does not have to deal with a new caregiver just before naptime, for example. Developmental milestones that the infant has already attained may suddenly disappear. An infant who was turning over and vocalizing before he went into the hospital for a month-long stay may not do so for weeks after this upsetting experience. A perceptive caregiver reassures a baby and lures him into trying old and new developmental tasks. Loving patience and persistence permit the infant to get back the courage needed to go on with early learnings.

What Do You Need to Know about Transitions from Toddlerhood?

Development is an active process. It involves alternating periods of relative calm with periods of tension and disorganization. While concentrating on perfecting body skills such as learning to walk without supports, an infant may temporarily decrease experimentation with babbling sounds. Inner bodily urges toward growth and mastery prompt exploration and discovery. But such growth may occur in spurts and consolidating periods, rather than in a steady, smooth progression. Forward advances and backward steps are very likely. Caregivers will need to be sensitive to signals that toddlers are ready for integration into preschool activities and settings. Not all toddlers are ready to move on at the same chronological age.

What are some of the signs that transitions will be appropriate? Certain gross criteria such as toileting controls or use of expressive (spoken) language are not necessarily the best. An early toilet-trained toddler may still need the support and security of a toddler playroom.

On the other hand, despite delays in language production, an intellectually advanced toddler with careful exploratory habits and long persistence at toy play may be a fine candidate. This child, quick to decode receptive (understood) language and respond correctly to suggestions, requests, and queries, may do very well when moved into a group of preschoolers who have several activity areas to choose from.

Some child care programs wish to advance toddlers as a group to new settings. But decisions are best made individually for each child in group care. Be aware that children who are not yet showing Piagetian Stage 6 mastery of object permanence games (see Piaget Task Checklist) may become very frustrated at certain preschool activities.

Asked to paste a magazine picture on the inside circle of a paper plate, a toddler kept peeling the picture from the plate. She was not disobedient, but she was puzzled about the disappearance of the blob of white library paste every time the picture was pressed down onto the plate. She was lifting the picture to check up on the paste. A caregiver who has some toddlers and some preschoolers in a mixed age group will need to be particularly sensitive to children who are intellectually in transition between sensorimotor learnings and early preoperational abilities. Some rules, sequences, sortings, and matchings may be quite confusing for toddlers who are just entering the preoperational period. Trainees need to discuss extensively what sensorimotor stages and early preoperational behaviors give more assurance that toddlers will fit comfortably in a mixed age group with preschoolers.

Some toddlers do need to be challenged by sophisticated materials, variety in programming, and places they can explore, climb, or balance upon. If capable of if-then reasonings, a richer world of water or sand play materials to pour, sift, drip, and contain should be provided. Toddlers in transition may enter with zest and experimentation into early science activities. Yet they may still be in diapers. Indeed, they may still forget a rule about not drinking from water play tubs.

Try out classification tasks with toddlers. If toddlers can sort toys or clothing or objects reliably into groups based on single criteria such as color, or shape, or belonging together (as foods or animals), or used together -- then these toddlers need more preschool experience. Matching and sorting games will nourish their growing classification abilities.

Can some toddlers line up orange juice cans from tallest to smallest or spoons from tiniest to biggest? These toddlers are ready for seriation games and activities more typical of preschool play.

Children teach us if we keep sharply alert to what they are doing. They show growing abilities to make sense of the world, to bring order into their world, and to communicate with others about experiences. As we notice their increased skills at role play, at understanding, at experimenting in organized ways with materials in order to find out "what happens if," we will have the best clues — child clues — that transitions from toddlerhood into the preschool play world are indeed at hand.

What Do You Need to Know about Assessing Your Own Caregiving?

Clinical observations. Babies are our best teachers. Their cues and communications give us feedback about the kind of caregiving job we are doing. Have trainees think aloud of all the bodily signs from head to toe that infants can give if they are either distressed or thriving in our care.

If infants are distressed, we notice rigid, tense muscles; whines, whimpers, cries, frowns; dull, vacant eyes; much spitting up; angry, thrashing limbs; disturbed sleep or bowel movements; nervous tension; repetitive acts such as head-banging; irritability; hesitant, fearful gestures; hurting of others by bites, hits, etc.; and lack of interest in exploratory or discovery play.

If infants are comfortable, secure, and interested, we notice calm faces; glistening, alert eyes; feeding and eating well; hands that reach out to explore, pat, pick up, and examine; bowels that move regularly with normal stools; limbs that make coordinated, vigorous motions; deep and restful sleep; bodies that mold trustingly onto a lap or shoulder; ability to be comforted by caregiver; and ability to play easily with toys if caregiver is nearby. The more we provide a nourishing, safe, predictable, yet interesting environment, the more babies will show thriving behaviors.

Checklist observations. Task checklists can be used to assess the kind and quality of caregiving efforts. Our Piaget Task Checklist, carried at the end of this book, has spaces for caregivers to monitor their own behavior with each infant for a month. A copy of this checklist for each infant assigned to a caregiver can be taped to the nursery wall. Caregivers can check off the Piagetian tasks done with each infant. What curricular activities have or have not been presented can be seen at a glance. Explain to trainees that items can be made available in two ways. Some can be presented as separate planned activities. Additionally, some Piagetian games can be easily integrated into the body care routines carried out daily with infants. How such games can be made part of daily routines is an important activity for caregivers to figure out. Call on your ingenuity and creativity in thinking up ideas together. Such object permanence activities as peek-a-boo, for example, are easy to play while washing or dressing an infant.

The ABC (Assessing the Behaviors of Caregivers) checklists (Honig and Lally 1973, 1975) can be used by a co-caregiver or supervisor to monitor specific adult interactions in seven areas: language facilitation, positive social-emotional inputs, negative social-emotional inputs, Piagetian sensorimotor skills and concept-development games, caregiving routines, room chores, and motoric inputs.

A single-page checklist of behaviors is available for caregivers of infants under 15-18 months (ABC I). Another single-page checklist (ABC II) is available for caregivers of older infants to 36 months. Samples are included at the back of this book.

Use ABC with trainees to develop a profile of caregiver behavior with infants (Honig and Lally 1975). Some caregivers will be talking a lot to infants, but they may perhaps need to increase reading to or singing to babies. Another caregiver presents a great many object permanence games, such as peek-a-boo and toy-hiding, but may need to increase presentation of toys that permit an infant to search for causal mechanisms, such as a handle to turn or a button to press to work a toy.

Some caregivers may arrange for interesting activities, but then they may fail to encourage or enjoy the social aspects of the games themselves so that infants lose interest and do not pursue the interaction with the materials or with the adult. Infants learn that they are okay and lovable during daily routine caregiving tasks and curricular activities. How a caregiver interacts should teach infants to be delighted and comfortable with themselves and about their explorations.

Talk with trainees about monitoring their own job stresses. Caregivers who are assigned too many infants or who receive too little assistance need to check their own feelings for possible burnout effects. If supervisors provide insufficient support or assistance at some crucial times, such as feeding and after-nap diapering, adult stress levels can increase. A good motto for infant caregivers is: "Keep a calm atmosphere to decrease stress all around."

In one center where hot food is delivered in styrofoam boxes, a caregiver soothingly reassured a young toddler who had trouble waiting for lunch. As the caregiver dished food onto all plates on the counter, she acknowledged the 13-month old's impatience: "I know you are really hungry, Jimmy. You wish lunch could be ready right now. I am putting meat loaf on your plate. The food is almost ready, Jimmy. Soon I will be able to serve your lunch." The young toddler, standing impatiently and moving his body near the caregiver who sent these reassuring messages, was helped. He was able to contain himself just enough. When his plate was put down, he slid onto his seat and dove into the food with both little hands! The co-caregiver had been toileting other infants. No one else was there to help. Reassuring calm tones permitted the baby to gain a bit of self-control and allowed the caregiver to serve the infants in her care without increasing stress in the environment.

Caregivers who are sensitive observers of themselves as well as sensitive responders to infant signals can better judge how their program is progressing. Be sure to go over the checklists carefully so that trainees feel comfortable with the meaning of each item to be checked off.

PIAGET TASK CHECKLIST

Please check the one(s) you did with the child today	NAME										BIRTHDATE									
	M	T	W	T	F	M	T	W	T	F	M	T	W	T	F	M	T	W	T	F
A. PREHENSION																				
1. Reaching for toys																				
2. Shaking toys																				
3. Suspended toys -- hitting																				
4. Suspended toys -- pulling																				
5. Squeaking toys																				
B. OBJECT PERFORMANCE																				
1. Peek-a-boo																				
2. Horizontal following of toy																				
3. Vertical screens -- hidden object																				
4. Horizontal screens -- visible displacement																				
5. Visible displacement -- 3 screens																				
6. Invisible displacement -- 1 screen																				
7. Invisible displacement -- 2 or 3 screens																				
8. (a) Put things in containers																				
(b) Nested boxes or bottles																				

PIAGET TASK CHECKLIST

Please check the one(s) you did with the child today	NAME					BIRTHDATE														
	M	T	W	T	F	M	T	W	T	F	M	T	W	T	F	M	T	W	T	F
C. MEANS AND ENDS																				
1. Reaching over obstacles																				
2. Use of the support																				
3. Pull horizontal string to get toy																				
4. Pull vertical string to get toy																				
5. Bunch chain into box																				
6. Use stick to get object																				
7. Reject solid ring for stack																				
D. NEW SCHEMAS																				
1. Hitting two objects together																				
2. Tactual patting, scratching																				
3. Examining objects																				
4. Sliding objects, such as car																				
5. Show something to someone																				
6. Adorn self -- put on necklace																				
7. Make doll or animal walk																				
8. Pull or stretch object																				
9. Attentive "listening" to songs																				

PIAGET TASK CHECKLIST

	NAME										BIRTHDATE										
Please check the one(s) you did with the child today	M	T	W	T	F		M	T	W	T	F		M	T	W	T	F		M	T	W	T	F
E. CAUSALITY																						
1. Bring unseen objects into sight																						
2. Ring bell to make sound																						
3. Wobble duck toy																						
4. Turn key to work toy																						
5. "Zoom" car to make it go																						
6. Work "Jack-in-the-box"																						
F. SPACE																						
1. Glance alternately																						
2. Find object by its sound																						
3. Vertical trajectory following																						
4. Reversed objects																						
5. Roll objects down plane																						
6. Use detour to get toys																						
G. IMITATION																						
1. Familiar visible "pat-a-cake"																						
2. Unfamiliar visible -- crook a finger																						
3. Familiar invisible -- wag head																						
4. Unfamiliar invisible -- eye wink																						

PIAGET TASK CHECKLIST

Please check the one(s) you did with the child today																					
NAME									**BIRTHDATE**												
	M	T	W	T	F	M	T	W	T	F	M	T	W	T	F	M	T	W	T	F
H. VERBAL LEARNING																					
1. Imitation of baby sounds																					
2. Unfamiliar sounds "la-la"																					
3. Labeling a) Objects																					
b) People																					
c) Feelings																					
d) Actions																					
4. Read stories																					
5. Verbal decoding																					
I. BALLET AND EXERCISES																					
1. Leg stretches																					
2. Roll body into ball																					
3. Rocking on stomach																					
4. Somersaults																					
5. Arms and legs apart and together																					
6. Bounce body to music																					
7. Bend to pick up																					
J. SOUNDS																					
1. Play xylophone or piano																					
2. Taped sounds																					
3. Listening to records																					
DAILY COMMENTS																					

ABC I
ASSESSING THE BEHAVIORS OF CAREGIVERS (WITH YOUNG INFANTS)

Caregiver's Name: _____   Rater: _____

Date _____ Day _____ Time _____

Child's Name																				
2-minute Trials																				
I. LANGUAGE FACILITATION																				
1. Elicits vocalization																				
2. Converses with child																				
3. Praises, encourages verbally																				
4. Offers help or solicitous remarks																				
5. Inquires of child or makes requests																				
6. Gives information or culture rules																				
7. Provides and labels sensory experience																				
8. Reads or shows pictures to child																				
9. Sings to or plays music for child																				
II. SOCIAL-EMOTIONAL: POSITIVE																				
1. Smiles at child																				
2. Uses raised, loving, or reassuring tones																				
3. Provides physical, loving contact																				
4. Plays social games with child																				
5. Eye contact to draw child's attention																				
III. SOCIAL-EMOTIONAL: NEGATIVE																				
1. Criticizes verbally, scolds, threatens																				
2. Forbids, negative demands																				
3. Frowns or restrains physically																				
4. Punishes physically																				
5. Isolates child physically — behavior modif.																				
6. Ignores child when child shows need for atten.																				

Copyright © 1973 by A. S. Honig and J. R. Lally

259

IV. PIAGETIAN TASKS																	
1. Object permanence																	
2. Means and ends																	
3. Imitation																	
4. Causality																	
5. Prehension: small-muscle skills																	
6. Space																	
7. New schemas																	
V. CAREGIVING: CHILD																	
1. Feeds																	
2. Diapers or toilets																	
3. Dresses or undresses																	
4. Washes or cleans child																	
5. Prepares child for sleep																	
6. Physical shepherding																	
7. Eye checks on child's well-being																	
VI. CAREGIVING: ENVIRONMENT																	
1. Prepares food																	
2. Tidies up room																	
3. Helps other caregiver(s)																	
VII. PHYSICAL DEVELOPMENT																	
1. Provides kinesthetic stimulation																	
2. Provides large-muscle play																	
VIII. DOES NOTHING																	

ABC II
ASSESSING THE BEHAVIORS OF CAREGIVERS (WITH OLDER INFANTS)

Caregiver's Name: _____ Rater: _____ Date _____ Day _____ Time _____

Place _____

I. FACILITATES LANGUAGE DEVELOPMENT															
1. Converses															
2. Models language															
3. Comments on Child's Remarks															
4. Praises, encourages															
5. Offers help, solicitous remarks, or makes verbal promises															
6. Inquires of child or makes request															
7. Gives information															
8. Gives culture rules															
9. Labels sensory experiences															
10. Reads or identifies pictures															
11. Sings or plays music with child															
12. Role-plays with child															
II. FACILITATES DEVELOPMENT OF SKILLS															
SOCIAL; PERSONAL: 1. Promotes child-child play (cog. & sensori.)															
2. Gets social games going															
3. Promotes self-help and social responsibility															
4. Helps child recognize his or her own needs															
5. Helps child delay gratification															
6. Promotes persistence, attention span															
PHYSICAL: 4. Small muscle, perceptual motor															
5. Large muscle, kinesthesis															
III. FACILITATES CONCEPT DEVELOPMENT															
1. Arranges learning of space and time															
2. Arranges learning of seriation, categorization, & polar concepts															
3. Arranges learning of number															
4. Arranges learning of physical causality															

IV. SOCIAL—EMOTIONAL: POSITIVE															
1. Smiles at child															
2. Uses raised, loving, or reassuring tones															
3. Provides physical, loving contact															
4. Uses eye contact to draw child's attention															
V. SOCIAL—EMOTIONAL: NEGATIVE															
1. Criticizes verbally, scolds, threatens															
2. Forbids, negative demands															
3. Frowns or restrains physically															
4. Isolates child physically —— behav. mod.															
5. Ignores child when child shows need for attention															
6. Punishes physically															
7. Gives attention to negative behavior which should be ignored															
VI. CAREGIVING —— BABY															
1. Diapers, toilets, dresses, washes, cleans															
2. Gives physical help, helps to sleep, shepherds															
3. Eye—checks on child's well-being															
4. Carries child															
VII. CAREGIVING: ENVIRONMENT															
1. Prepares/serves food															
2. Tidies up room															
3. Helps other caregiver(s)															
4. Prepares activities, arranges environment to stimulate child															
VIII. QUALITATIVE CATEGORIES															
1. Encourages creative expression															
2. Matches "tempo" and/or developmental level of child															
3. Actively engages child's interest in activity or activity choice															
5. Follows through on requests, promises, directions, discipline															
IX. DOES NOTHING															

Use red pencil to tally caregiver behavior with boys
Use black pencil to tally caregiver behavior with girls

BIBLIOGRAPHY

Ainsworth, M. "Social Development in the First Year of Life: Maternal Influences on Infant-Mother Attachment." In J. M. Tanner, ed., Developments in Psychiatric Research: Essays Based on the Sir Geoffrey Vickers Lectures of the Mental Health Foundation. London: Hodder & Stoughton, 1977. Mothering patterns differ for securely attached, ambivalent, and avoidant babies. Maternal sensitivity to infant signals, as indicated by prompt responsiveness to crying, encouragement of face-to-face interactions, and tender careful handling, was most significant as a predictor of secure attachment. These babies responded positively to close bodily contact, were more compliant, and were more willing to move off into exploratory play.

The American Baby 42, no. 14 (mid-July 1980).

Ames, L. B., and O. Ilg. Your Two-Year Old, Terrible or Tender. New York: Dell, 1976. Clear descriptions are given of every nuance of toddler behavior in all areas of development so that a caregiver will know well the disconcerting difficulties and the delights of this age group in order to provide loving care. This is a very difficult age to handle; this book helps a caregiver or parent live through it.

Beckwith, L. "Relationships Between Attributes of Mothers and Their Infants' IQ Scores." Child Development 42 (1971): 1083-97. Adoptive infants' IQ scores were related to how much the mothers spoke to and touched infants and gave them opportunities to explore the house. Fewer such maternal behaviors correlated with lower Cattell scores.

Birns, B., and M. Golden, "Prediction of Intellectual Performance at Three Years from Infant Tests." Merrill Palmer Quarterly (1972). Black infants from middle-class families showed a more than 20 IQ point advantage over welfare infants by three years of age. The effects of patterns of family interactions and language are discussed as possible factors in this large social-class difference evident by the end of the infancy period, but not early in infancy.

Bower, T. G. R. A Primer of Infant Development. San Francisco: Freeman, 1977. Research results throw light on emerging infant motoric and language skills, interpersonal communication patterns, and concept development. Photographs nicely illustrate the early emergence of many infant understandings.

Brazelton, T. Berry. Infants and Mothers: Differences in Development. New York: Delacorte, 1969. The lives of three babies — active, average, and quiet — illustrate the widely divergent patterns of behavior of normal infants in families during the first year of life.

-----. Toddlers and Parents: A Declaration of Independence. New York: Dell, 1974.

Bromwich, R. Working with Parents and Infants, an Interactional Approach. Baltimore: University Park Press, 1981.

-----. "Stimulation in the First Year of Life? A Perspective on Infant Development." Young Children (January 1977).

Bronfenbrenner, U. "Is Early Intervention Effective?" Paper delivered at the National Association for the Education of Young Children, Atlanta, Georgia, November 1972.

Caldwell, B. M. How Babies Learn. 1966, 35 minutes, New York University Film Library. The tasks and advances of each quarter of the first year of life are graphically illustrated.

-----. Nurturing. Davidson Films, 3701 Buchanan Street, San Francisco, Calif. 94123.

-----. "The Rationale for Early Intervention." Exceptional Children 36 (1970): 717-26.

Caldwell, B. M., and J. Richmond. "The Children's Center in Syracuse, New York." In L. L. Dittmann, ed., Early Child Care: The New Perspectives. New York: Atherton, 1968.

Caldwell, B. M., and L. E. Smith. "Day Care for the Very Young — Prime Opportunity for Primary Prevention." American Journal of Public Health 60, no. 4 (1970): 690-97.

Caldwell, B. M., and D. J. Stedman, eds. Infant Education: A Guide for Helping Handicapped Children in the First Three Years. New York: Walker, 1977. Training programs to assist infants with handicaps are described in detail by the various contributors to this volume.

Caldwell, B., C. M. Wright, A. S. Honig, and J. Tannenbaum. "Infant Day Care and Attachment." American Journal of

Orthopsychiatry 40 (1970): 397–412. A group of home–reared children and a group of children who had been enrolled in an infant day care center were examined at 30 months of age for differences in child–mother and mother–child attachment patterns. Essentially, no differences could be detected. However, an association was found between strength of attachment and developmental level of child, and between strength of attachment and amount of stimulation/support for development available in the home.

Carew, J., I. Chan, and C. Halfar. Observing Intelligence in Young Children. Englewood Cliffs, N.J.: Prentice–Hall, 1976. Eight case studies of young children from diverse family backgrounds are described to illuminate the striking differences in intellectual development of the children. Fourteen ways that mothers of well–developed children influence their child's experience are focussed on in chapter three.

DeVilliers and DeVilliers. Out of the Mouths of Babes. 1978, 30 minutes, Film–makers Library, 290 West End Avenue, New York, N.Y.

Dittman, L. The Infants We Care For. Washington, D.C.: National Association for the Education of Young Children, 1973. For day care workers of infants and toddlers this book covers such areas as working with the family, practical considerations for operating a center, selection and training of staff, and evaluation of staff.

–––––. What We Can Learn from Infants. Washington, D.C.: National Association for the Education of Young Children, 1970.

Elardo, R., and B. Pagan, eds. Perspectives on Infant Day Care. Little Rock, Ark.: Southern Association for Children Under Six, Box 5403, Brady Station, Ark. 72205. This excellent collection of articles aids infant day care staff in conceptualizing program, in creating a healthy, safe, and attractive environment for care, and in planning program to serve the developmental needs of infants.

Escalona, S. K. Object Permanence, Spatial Relationships, and Causality. New York University Film Library, New York, N.Y. These three films depict testing of Piagetian development of infants 4 to 22 months.

Evans, E. B., and G. E. Saia. Day Care for Infants: The Case for Infant Day Care and a Practical Guide. This book presents a case for infant day care and then offers specific advice on licensing requirements, preparing a budget and raising funds, locating a center site, ordering equipment and toys, and preparing food.

Fitzgerald, A. E., S. Ledesma, W. Swarthout, and A. Parker. Orientation Manual for Trainees in Infant–Toddler Day Care. Report No. 2. Infant Toddler Day Care Project, Early Childhood Research Institute for Family & Child Research, College of Human Ecology, Michigan State University, 1972.

Flint, B. The Flint Infant Security Scale. Guidance Centre, 1974. The Governing Council of the University of Toronto, Toronto, Canada M4W2K8. A behavior rating scale designed to assess the mental health of children from birth to two years of age.

Fowler, W. Guides to Early Day Care and Teaching. Toronto, Canada: Ontario Institute for Studies in Education, 1978. Three guides for basic care, free play, and guided child learning provide practical methods and materials, concepts, and techniques that caregivers will find useful.

Fraiberg, S. H. "The First Eighteen Months," and "Eighteen Months to Three Years." In The Magic Years. New York: Scribner's, 1959.

–––––. "Intervention in Infancy: A Program for Blind Infants." Journal of the American Academy of Child Psychiatry 10, no. 3 (1971): 381–405.

Fraiberg, S., E. Adelson, and V. Shapiro. "Ghosts in the Nursery: A Psychoanalytic Approach to Impaired Infant–Mother Relationships." Journal of the American Academy of Child Psychiatry 14 (1975): 387–421.

Frankenburg, W. K., and J. B. Dodds. The Denver Developmental Screening Test –– Manual. 1968. Ladoca Project and Publishing Fdtn., East 51st St. and Lincoln St., Denver, Colo. 80216. This quick screening test is easy for child care staff to learn and use. Poor scores alert caregivers to the need for more thorough developmental testing and possible remediation.

Friedlander, B. L., G. Sterritt, and G. Kirk. Exceptional Infant, Vol. 3 Assessment & Intervention. New York: Bruner/Mazel, 1975. This collection of articles on assessment and intervention strategies links three areas in child development –– problems of developmentally disabled children with more or less readily identifiable special needs, concern and programs for minority or disadvantaged children, and issues of developmental assessment.

Frost, J. Understanding and Nurturing Infant Development. Washington, D.C.: Association for Childhood Education International, 1976. Information on infant intervention programs, day care, parent-infant relations, and on infant competence is succinctly summarized.

Geisy, R. A Guide for Home Visitors. Nashville, Tenn.: DARCEE, George Peabody College for Teachers, 1970.

George, C., and M. Main. "Social Interactions of Young Abused Children: Approach, Avoidance, and Aggression." Child Development 50 (1979): 306-518. Ten abused toddlers (1-3 years) in day care more frequently than matched controls from stressed families exhibited the following behaviors in day care — harassed their caregivers, assaulted their peers, less often approached caregivers in response to friendly overtures, more often avoided peers or adults.

Glickman, B. and N. Springer. Who Cares for the Baby? New York: Schocken, 1978. This sensible, clear look at what infants and mothers need in order to thrive well surveys alternate infant care arrangements and should be helpful to families trying to choose family day care, group day care, home care, or other arrangements.

Golden, M., B. Birns, W. Bridger, and B. Moss. "Social-Class Differentiation in Cognitive Development among Black Preschool Children." Child Development 42 (1971): 37-45. IQ difference larger than 20 points were found between black infants from middle class compared to welfare families.

Gonzales-Mena, J., and D. Eyer. Infancy and Caregiving. Palo Alto, Calif.: Mayfield, 1980. The development of attachment and the caregiver-infant relationship is central to this curriculum guide. Anecdotes are plentiful. A chart included in the Appendix provides ideas for organizing the infant's physical environment to stimulate different areas of development.

Gordon, I. Baby Learning through Baby Play. New York: St. Martin's, 1970. These practical guides to developing parent-infant interaction in the first twelve months view child-rearing as a partnership. Suggestions are given for observing and adapting to an infant's rhythms and for ways to develop infant responsiveness.

Greenfield, P., and E. Tronick. Infant Curriculum. The Bromley-Health Guide to the Care of Infants in Groups. Rev. ed. Santa Monica: Goodyear, 1980. Discussions of goals, values, and discipline techniques as well as an overview of infant development and suggestions for daily schedule make this a practical guide for group care.

Heber, R., and H. Garber. "The Milwaukee Project: A Study of the Use of Family Intervention to Prevent Cultural Familial Mental Retardation." In B. Z. Friedlander, G. M. Sterritt, and G. E. Kirk, eds. Exceptional Infant. Vol. 3. New York: Bruner/Mazel, 1975. Mean IQ scores of infants in an enriched infant program from 3 months on (tutorial at first) differed from controls by more than 20 points after 5 years in program. The infants' mothers had a WAIS score of less than 75. Cultural familial retardation can be prevented.

Herbert-Jackson, E., et al. The Infant Center: A Complete Guide to Organizing and Managing an Infant Day Care. Baltimore: University Park Press, 0000.

The High/Scope Press. Your Baby's Day. 600 North River Street, Ypsilanti, Michigan, 48197. Telephone 313-485-2000. Audiovision

Honig, A. S. "Current Research in Infant Development." Bulletin for the Montessori Society (December 1979). Recent research findings in 10 infancy areas, such as maternal-infant bonding, competent fathering, biological and drug factors, and effects of intervention projects are summarized in nontechnical style.

-----. "Curriculum for Infants in Day Care." Child Welfare 53, no. 10 (1974): An integrated curriculum combining Piagetian, Eriksonian, and language developmental principles suggests specific activities and positive ways of interacting socially with infants while presenting activities.

-----. "The Developmental Needs of Infants: How Can They be Met in a Day Care Setting?" Dimensions 2, no. 2 (1974).

-----. "Training Caregivers to Provide Loving Learning Experiences for Babies." Dimensions 6 (1978): 33-43.

-----. "What are the Needs of Infants?" Young Children (1981).

-----. "What You Need to Know to Select and Train Your Day Care Staff." Child Care Quarterly 8 (1979): 19-35.

Honig, A. S., and J. R. Lally. "How Good is Your Infant Program? Use an Observation Method to Find Out." Child Care Quarterly 1 (1975): 194-207.

-----. Infant Caregiving: A Design for Training. 2nd ed. Syracuse: Syracuse University Press, 1981. This basic handbook is designed to help train caregivers to meet infants' developmental needs in group care. In practical language, and with dozens of pictures, numerous activities are recommended. Many extra topics are covered, such as the human qualities of caregivers, space and equipment use, communicating with families, record keeping, mainstreaming handicapped infants, and assessing caregiver and infant progress.

Huntington, D. S., S. Provence, and R. K. Parker. Day Care 2: Serving Infants. OCD Day Care Series. Washington, D.C.: USGPO, 1972. Principles of infant day care, organization of day care and activities for infants are provided in clear, easy to read terms that are helpful for daily planning.

Illingworth, R. S. "The Predictive Value of Development Tests in the First Year with Special Reference to the Diagnosis of Mental Subnormality." Journal of Child Psychiatry and Psychology (1961): 210–13. When clinical judgments are added to developmental assessment then a diagnosis of mental inferiority made in the first year of life predicts IQ scores in the early grades with 75 percent accuracy.

John Tracy Clinic. Getting Your Baby Ready to Talk: Home Study Plan. Los Angeles, Calif. 90007. A correspondence course for parents of infants from 6 to 18 months of age is available for the motivation of early hearing and language skills.

Johnson & Johnson. Infant Developmental Program: Birth to 12 Months. New Brunswick, N.J.: Johnson & Johnson, 1976. Curricular exercises are provided with profuse and clear photographs to enable parents to enrich their baby's development through ordinary care routines as well as provision of special learning opportunities. The importance of the emotional element between caregiver and infant is emphasized beautifully.

Johnson, Vicki, and R. Werner. A Step-by-Step Learning Guide for Retarded Infants and Children. Syracuse, N.Y.: Syracuse University Press, 1975. Written for retarded children who have a functional level of less than four years of age, this book includes checklists and curriculum tasks in the areas of gross motor, self-care, language, fine motor, and perception.

Jones, S. Good Things for Babies: A Catalogue and Sourcebook of Safety and Consumer Advice about Products Needed During the First 24 Months of Babylife. Boston: Houghton-Mifflin, 1976. This catalog of toys and equipment for babies with where-to-buy suggestions also includes good tips on safety in toys.

Kagan, J. "Do Infants Think?" Scientific American 226, no. 3 (1972): 74–82. Cognitive development, as measured by attention to discrepant stimuli and by hypothesis formation and anticipation, has been found to begin as early as nine months of age.

Kagan, J., R. Kearsley, and P. Zelazo. Infancy. Cambridge, Mass.: Harvard University Press, 1978. Early experience and infant development research findings are discussed. The results of an infant day care program are reported. The development of three dozen 3-to-30-month-old Chinese and Caucasian infants in group day care was not found to differ with respect to play, language, cognitive development, or social interactions from a matched group of home-reared infants.

Kagan, J., and X. Gardner. Infancy. Film, 21 minutes, New York: Harper & Row, 1972.

Kaplan, H. Oneness and Separateness: From Infant to Individual. New York: Simon & Schuster, 1978. Writing with poetic sensitivity and clinical insights into infant personality developments, Dr. Kaplan interprets Mahler's Theory that infants must balance optimally between urges to mold oneness with the caregiver and opposite strivings to become a separate self from the adult. The see-sawing needs of infants require perceptive and generous caregiver understanding and actions.

Karnes, M. B., J. A. Teska, A. S. Hodgins, and E. D. Badger. "Educational Intervention at Home by Mothers of Disadvantaged Infants." Child Development 41 (1970): 925–35.

Keister, M. "The Good Life" for Infants and Toddlers: Group Care of Infants. 2nd ed. Washington, D.C.: National Association for the Education of Young Children, 1977. "Quality care" in the Demonstration Nursery Center, University of North Carolina, is depicted with delightful pictures and thought-provoking text. The revised edition includes an updated reference list.

—————. Guidelines for Budgeting Infant Care Programs. Greensboro, N.C.: University of North Carolina, 1970.

Kilmer, S. "Infant–Toddler Group Day Care: A Review of Research." In L. Katz, ed. Current Topics in Early Childhood Education, Vol. 2. New Jersey: Ablex, 1979.

Klaus, M. H., T. Legern, and M. A. Trause, eds. Maternal Attachment and Mothering Disorders.

Piscataway, N.J.: Johnson & Johnson Baby Products, 1979.

Lally, J. R., and I. J. Gordon. _Learning Games for Infants and Toddlers_. Syracuse, N.Y.: New Readers Press, 1977. A series of increasingly advanced games are provided for parents with babies from 2 months to 2 years. Each game specifies the position, action, purpose of the game, and expansions on the game.

Lally, J. R., A. S. Honig, and B. M. Caldwell. "Training Paraprofessionals for Work with Infants and Toddlers." _Young Children_ 28, no. 3 (1973): 173–82. Presentation and creation of sensorimotor materials and activities, language and motoric games, use of audiovisual teaching aids, role-playing techniques, and in-classroom supervised experiences are among the specific training suggestions offered.

Lally, J. R., and A. S. Honig. "The Family Development Research Program: A Program for Prenatal, Infant, and Early Childhood Enrichment." In M. C. Day and R. D. Parker, eds. _The Preschool in Action: Exploring Early Childhood Programs_. 2nd ed. Boston: Allyn & Bacon, 1977. This detailed description of a combined infant-toddler quality day care plus parent-home visitation program is enriched with reports on positive changes in children's functioning through participation.

Lambie, D. Z., J. T. Bond, and D. P. Weikart. "Home Teaching with Mother and Infants." Ypsilanti, Mich.: High Scope Education Research Foundation, 1974. An in-home program of Piagetian developmental games mothers can play with infants is described.

Language Development. Color film, 20 minutes, 1972. Available from Washington State University, Audio-visual center, Pullman, Wash. This film covers the early months of crying, cooing, and babbling. The importance of the child's capacities to learn language and the environment are discussed.

Leach, P. _Babyhood_. New York: Knopf, 1976. To provide detailed portrayal of the behaviors, needs, and feelings of a developing child, this book is divided into five sections: the first 6 weeks; 6 weeks to 3 months; 3 to 6 months; 6 months to one year; and the second year. Within each section topics such as feeding, sleeping, elimination, managing his or her body, language, perception, play, fears, and phobias are covered.

Levenstein, P. "Verbal Interaction Project/ Mother-Child Home Program." _Manual for Replication of the Mother-Child Home Program_. 2nd ed. Freeport, N.Y.: Demonstration Project, 1973. This manual explains how to carry out a home visitation model to provide toddlers and parents with toys and books (VISMs — Verbal, Interaction Stimulus Materials) with which they can enrich their children's development.

Lief, N. R. _The First Year of Life: A Curriculum for Parenting Education_. New York: Keyway, 1979. This really practical how-to book answers parents' questions about every aspect of caring for, playing with, and reading to a baby.

Lischner, K., N. Spotts, and M. Young. _Developmental Play as a Learning Tool — Birth to Three Years: Curriculum Guide for Infant-Toddler Educational Program_. Glassboro, N.J.: Glassboro State College Early Childhood Demonstration Center, 1975. This infant-centered curriculum explores ideas for activities that can be provided for infants as they enter different developmental phases such as "What would happen if . . . ," "I am me and you are you," and "Things sure look different up here."

McCall, R. B. _Infants_. Cambridge, Mass.: Harvard University Press, 1979. This practical book for parents and caregivers provides an understandable review of research on infant development and parent-infant interaction.

McDiarmid, N., M. Peterson, and J. Sutherland. _Loving and Learning, Interacting with Your Child from Birth to Three_. New York: Harcourt Brace Jovanovich, 1975. The importance of warm and affectionate adult-child interrelationships for the child's learning and intellectual development is emphasized. Each chapter, dealing with successive 6-month periods of life from birth to age 3, includes an overview of the infant's stage of development, major changes that take place during that period, and many pleasurable activities for caregiver and child together.

Marzolla, Jean. _Supertot: Creative Learning Activities for Children One to Three and Sympathetic Advice for Their Parents_. New York: Harper & Row, 1977. Light-hearted learning activities that supertots are sure to like are well illustrated.

Neugebauer, R., and R. Lurie, eds. _Caring for Infants and Toddlers: What Works, What Doesn't_. Summit Child Care Center, 1980. _Order from Child Care Information Exchange_, 70 Oakley Road, Belmont, Mass. 02178. This book of readings focusses on five areas: (1) how to develop an appropriate curriculum,

(2) how to select and train staff, (3) how to maintain effective parent relations, (4) how to meet young children's caretaking needs, and (5) how to design the environment.

Osofsky, J. D. Handbook of Infant Development. New York: John Wiley, 1979. This volume is a comprehensive and scholarly compilation of new ideas, conceptualizations, and research in the area of infancy. Theoretical, methodological, conceptual, intervention, and clinical issues are considered.

Painter, G. Teach Your Baby. New York: Simon & Schuster, 1971.

Palmer, F., and R. Siegel. "Minimal Intervention at Ages Two and Three and Subsequent Intellective Changes." In M. Day and R. Parkes, eds. The Preschool in Action, 2nd ed. Boston: Allyn and Bacon, 1977. A tutorial program that focussed on teaching specific concepts (such as wet-dry) to black male toddlers showed significantly higher achievements for children who had participated compared to controls.

Parke, R. D. "Perspectives on Father-Infant Interaction." In J. D. Osofsky, ed., Handbook of Infant Development. New York: Wiley-Interscience, 1979. A survey of research literature on fathering suggests that fathers are attractive play partners who provide different kinds of experiences from mother for babies.

Piaget, J. The Origins of Intelligence in Children. New York: International Universities Press, 1952.

Pierson, D. "Brookline Early Education Program." M. A. Project Reports, 1973, 1974. An interdisciplinary program of developmental information, social support, and medical services was provided for families by pediatricians, social service, and child development personnel working together.

Pines, M. "Good Samaritans at Age Two?" Psychology Today 13, no. 1 (1979): 66-77. Research by M. Yarrow and Zahn-Waxler suggests that infants in the second year of life exhibit empathetic concern for others' distress. Caregivers boost altruistic learning by expressing firm disapproval of hurtful acts and real concern for the victim of a toddler's assault plus showing much love and concern for the toddler in everyday life situations.

Pizzo, P. The Infant Day Care Debate: Not Whether but How. Washington, D.C.: Day Care and Child Development Council of America, 1978. Eight different kinds of child care arrangements that parents currently make for very young children are examined for advantages and disadvantages related to the qualities that parents look for in infant day care.

Prescott, E., E. Jones, and S. Kritchevsky. Assessment of Child-Rearing Environments: An Ecological Approach. Pasedena, Calif.: Pacific Oaks College, 1971. Dimensions of the environment are identified which are helpful in assessing an environment's pertinence, richness, and adequacy for children with diverse developmental and social histories.

Provence, S. Guide for the Care of Infants in Groups. New York: Child Welfare League of America, 1975. The emotional relationship of babies to people who care for them is stressed throughout the chapters on feeding, bowel and bladder control, sleep, etc. A section on developmental landmarks permits group caregivers to assess how well babies are progressing.

Pushaw, D. Teach Your Child to Talk: A Parent Handbook. Albany, N.Y.: State Education Department, Office for Education of Children with Handicapping Conditions, Special Education Instructional Materials Center, 1975. Developmental questions are raised and activities are suggested to help caregivers stimulate language understanding and expression in infants, toddlers, and preschoolers.

Rabinowitz, M., G. Weiner, and C. R. Jackson. In the Beginning: A Parent Guide to Activities and Experiences for Infants from Birth to Six Months. New Orleans: New Orleans Parent Child Development Center, 1973.

Ramsey, C. T., and F. A. Campbell. "Compensatory Education for Disadvantaged Children." School Review 87, no. 2 (1979): 171-89. By 48 months experimental infants achieved a mean Stanford-Binet score of 93.4 compared to the randomly selected control group infants' mean score of 81.3.

Reilly, A. P., ed. The Communication Game. Piscataway, N.J.: Johnson & Johnson Baby Products, 1980.

Rubenstein, J. L., and C. Howes. "Caregiver and Infant Behavior in Day Care and in Homes." Developmental Psychology 15 (1979): 1-24. Mothers held babies less than did caregivers in centers. There was significantly more peer interaction in the center than in the home.

Schaefer, E., and M. Aaronson. "Infant Education Research Project: Implementation and Implications of a Home Tutoring Program."

In M. Day and R. Parker, eds. <u>The Preschool in Action</u>. Boston: Allyn and Bacon, 1977. An in-home program that targeted year-old black infants for tutorial enrichment found strong IQ gains at 36 months. The gains "washed out" three years later, possibly because of lack of specific parental involvement.

Segal, M. <u>From Birth to One Year</u> and <u>From One to Two Years</u>. Nova University Series, 1976. B. L. Winch & Associates, 45 Hitching Post Dr., Bldg. 2, Rolling Hills Estates, Calif. 90274. These two brief curricula guides present activities that parents can carry out with infants.

Segner, L., and C. Patterson. <u>Ways to Help Babies Grow and Learn</u>. Denver, Colo.: World Press, 1970.

Smart, M., and R. Smart, eds. <u>Infants -- Development and Relationships</u>. New York: Macmillan, 1973. Infancy is discussed with regard to (1) prenatal development and birth, (2) early infancy, (3) emerging resources for coping with the world, and (4) relationships with people. A number of readings for each area is included.

Smith, R., ed. <u>Introduction to Infant Stimulation: A Training Manual</u>. Rockhill: Winthrop College, University of South Carolina, 1976. Objectives, procedures, and materials appropriate for infant stimulation program are spelled out in precise detail. Suggestions are offered for teaching self-help skills and holding parent conferences.

Sparling, J., and I. Lewis. <u>Learning Games for the First Three Years: A Guide to Parent/Child Play</u>. New York: Walker, 1979. One hundred games reflecting typical patterns of infant development are introduced with a checklist which shows the main learning theme of each game and on which the child's progress can be recorded.

Spitz, R. <u>Grief: A Peril in Infancy</u>. This black and white film is narrated by Dr. Spitz. Clear examples are presented of the deep sorrow and developmental regression that may occur when babies are suddenly deprived of the mothers and mothering which has supported their early growth. Univ. of Pa.

Sroupe, A. <u>Knowing and Enjoying your Baby</u>. Englewood Cliffs, N.J.: Prentice-Hall, 1977. The growth of smiling, laughter, joy, fear of the unfamiliar, and other emotions is described so that a sensitive caregiver can learn to be responsive to baby's signals and to interact and play games. The growth of reciprocal loving is facilitated by a caregiver attentive to cooperative ways of relating with baby.

Stayton, D. J., R. Hogan, and M. D. S. Ainsworth. "Infant Obedience and Maternal Behavior. The Origins of Socialization Reconsidered." <u>Child Development</u> 42 (1971): 1057-69. Mothers who are sensitive to infant signals, provide body cuddling, and allow floor freedom for exploration have more obedient babies.

Stone, J. G. <u>A Guide to Discipline</u>. Rev. ed. Washington, D.C.: National Association for the Education of Young Children, 1978. Helping children learn to control their own behavior and learning skilled ways of talking with children are focussed on in this book.

Stone, L. J., and J. Church. See chapters on "The Infants" and "The Toddlers" in <u>Childhood and Adolescence</u>. New York: Random House, 1979. These admirably written descriptions of normal infant and toddler development should be very useful in helping caregivers understand the whole child under the age of three.

Stone, L. J., H. T. Smith, and L. B. Murphy. <u>The Competent Infant: Research and Commentary</u>. New York: Basic Books, 1973. This compendium of infancy research findings should prove helpful background reading.

Trotter, S., and E. B. Thomas, eds. <u>Social Responsiveness of Infants</u>. Piscataway, N.J.: Johnson & Johnson Baby Products, 1978.

Upchurch, B. <u>Easy-to-Do Toys and Activities for Infants and Toddlers</u>. Demonstration Project: Group Care of Infants, University of North Carolina at Greensboro, 1971.

Uzgiris, I. C., ed. <u>Social Interaction and Communication during Infancy</u>. San Francisco: Jossey-Boss, 1979. The authors present initial findings from research that uses the infant as a full participant in interpersonal interactions and views mothering in terms of a dialog engaged in with the infant.

Uzgiris, I. C., and J. McV. Hunt. Champaign, Ill.: University of Illinois. Ordinal scales of infant psychological development. Six reels, 1967: (1) object permanence, (2) development of means, (3) imitation: gestural and vocal, (4) operational causality, (5) object relations in space, and (6) development of schemas. Visual Aids Service, Division of University Extension, University of Illinois, Champaign, Ill. 61820

White, B. *The First Three Years of Life*. Englewood Cliffs, N.J.: Prentice-Hall, Inc., 1975.

Willerman, L., S. H. Broman, and M. Fiedler "Infant Development, Preschool IQ, and Social Development." *Child Development* 41, no. 1 (1970): 69-79. Infants with low developmental scores during the first year are significantly more likely to be developmentally delayed if reared in families of low socioeconomic status. No such correlation was found for infants reared in enriched family environments.

Willis, A., and H. Riccuiti. *A Good Beginning for Babies. Guidelines for Group Care*. Washington, D.C.: National Association for the Education of Young Children, 1975. Goals and principles, relations with families, program and staff organization, play and learning, helping babies adjust, routine caregiving, staff composition and training, physical space and equipment, health and safety are topics covered. Appendices include personality rating scales and checklists of developmental landmarks.

Yarrow, L. J., J. L. Rubenstein and F. A. Pedersen. *Infant and Environment: Early Cognitive and Motivational Development*. Washington, D.C.: Hemisphere, 1975.